THE BORISAURUS

THE
BORISAURUS

THE DICTIONARY OF
BORIS JOHNSON

SIMON WALTERS

Biteback Publishing

First published in Great Britain in 2020 by
Biteback Publishing Ltd
Westminster Tower
3 Albert Embankment
London SE1 7SP
Copyright © Simon Walters 2020

ISBN 978-1-78590-569-8

10 9 8 7 6 5 4 3 2 1

A CIP catalogue record for this book is available from the British Library.

Set in Minion Pro

Printed and bound in Great Britain by
CPI Group (UK) Ltd, Croydon CR0 4YY

INTRODUCTION

I t was in August 2008 that I first experienced Latinate
evasion; I had no idea what it was at the time. I didn't
find out until more than ten years later while researching
this book. According to this technique, if you are backed
into a corner and called upon to give a straight answer,
there is a way out: give a Latin veneer to your response
and people will be so impressed or bedazzled that they
won't notice that you have both given and withheld an
answer at one and the same time.

Most won't even know what you are talking about until
later, when they have googled it, which is the position
I was in after an interview at the 2008 Olympic Games
in Beijing. I was reporting on Prime Minister Gordon
Brown's visit, but Boris Johnson stole the headlines as the
newly elected Mayor of London, mainly with his startling
speech marking London as the host of the next Games.

'Wiff-waff' was coming home, he declared, stating that
the Chinese national sport of ping-pong was invented in
England by the Victorians. I was in the audience and saw
the collective jaws of the dignitaries alongside him hit

the floor in astonishment that anyone, especially a relative political novice, could be so irreverent on such a grand occasion – and carry it off.

The Latinate evasion came twenty-four hours earlier, when I interviewed Johnson at the Games. With his Old Etonian rival David Cameron yet to make his mark as Tory leader, the obvious way to skewer the new mayor was to ask if his sights were now set on the Conservative leadership.

After playfully dodging the question once or twice, Johnson muttered: 'Were I to be pulled like Cincinnatus from my plough, it would be a great privilege...' and sauntered off.

Come again?

After getting a wifi connection I learned that Cincinnatus was a Roman statesman of great virtue who had given up public life but returned from his farm to save Rome from invasion. The denarius dropped: Boris did want to oust Dave. I had my story. But Johnson had couched his disloyalty in such heroic lyricism it made you want to smile, not scowl; to admire his ambition and erudition, not admonish him. It appears he learned this device from one of his Tory idols, Alan Clark, a minister in Margaret Thatcher's government.

It is not hard to see why Johnson might identify with right-wing intellectual Clark, who was notorious for calling Africa 'Bongo Bongo Land' and parading affairs with the wife of a judge and her two daughters, whom he referred to as 'the coven'. But what struck Johnson most was Clark's response when he was caught lying in the 1990s arms-to-Iraq weapons scandal. When asked in court if he had told the truth, Clark drawled that he had been 'economical with the *actualité*'.

It wasn't just 'brilliant', concluded Johnson, speaking at a Latin-themed charity event in 2007; it was 'also less self-condemnatory than "I lied". The thing about Latinate words is they're evasive.' Eureka.

Classicist Johnson's articles, speeches, books and interviews are full of the lexicon and imagery of gods, myths, battles and epic poems adapted for schoolboy puns and scholarly polemics. They are also full of German, Norse, Yiddish and many other languages, to inform and entertain – as well as to get him out of a tight corner. It is hard not to be impressed by the vast cultural hinterland he flaunts; his range of voices, from Archimedes to Alf Garnett, Suetonius to the Stones, grandiloquent prose and grimace-inducing wordplays delivered together on great occasions.

One minute he is Billy Bunter, all 'cripes' and 'crumbs'; the next, Mary Beard retracing the Battle of Cannae; then it is a cod Churchill, replacing the V for victory with a walrus-like, flapping Benny Hill salute. Next it is Jeremy Clarkson on Viagra bellowing over the roar of an MG roadster. In one bound he can leap from Gussie Fink-Nottle to a Keef Richards riff; adolescent to academic, philosopher to fool without pausing for breath.

An article about motoring speed limits contains what

seems like an innocuous reference to a Ferrari 'Testadicazzo'. Not being familiar with that model – nor an Italian speaker – I checked. The result is outrageous: you will find it in this book under 'T'.

The impact of Johnson's controversial statements is often heightened by masking them with a 'miasma of faux ignorance', as one commentator put it. He gains the attention of those with little interest in politics by inviting them to laugh at him playing the buffoon – because they can see that underneath it, he isn't one. He calls it 'imbecilio' (another favourite Latin word).

Latinate evasion hasn't always got him off the hook. When the story of his affair with Petronella Wyatt broke in 2004, I was the political journalist who asked him if it was true. His reply, dismissing it as an 'inverted pyramid of piffle', will live for ever as the original 'Borisism'.

It may have been 'brilliant', but it was also a lie. He was fired from the Tory front bench as a result. Johnson looked on the bright side: 'There are no disasters, only opportunities. And, indeed, opportunities for fresh disasters.'

The range, roots, richness and rudery of the nouns, verbs and adjectives at his command is spellbinding. When he can't find the right word, he makes one up.

If you constructed a giant word map based on Johnson's writings, among the names of Homer, Pericles, Caesar, Antony and Cleopatra, Thatcher, Bush, Blair, Brown, Delors, Trump, Cameron, May, Corbyn and Heseltine, there would be all manner of descriptions of breasts, male virility and sex in general. Listen to his defiant tribute to Dr Samuel Johnson, who produced one of the first English dictionaries: a 'slobbering, sexist xenophobe who understood human nature'; a man who, despite his 'flobbery lips', had such 'natural charisma' that women fought to sit next to him; a 'brilliant champion of the English language and the little guy'. Which Johnson does he have in mind?

Some of his earlier work (in particular his novel, the unsubtly titled *Seventy-Two Virgins*) is shocking when reviewed in the third decade of the twenty-first century. Parts seem like an excuse for the racist and sexist out-pourings you might expect from the 1970s teenage public schoolboy he once was, except it was written in 2004, when he was entering his forties and had been an MP for three years. The word 'coon' appears gratuitously six times within a few sentences – admittedly as part of the dialogue, not, strictly speaking, the voice of the narrator; but there is no mistaking it as coming from a place of authenticity. It is the same streak that made him dare to joke about Muslim women with 'letter-box' veils resem-bling 'bank robbers' less than a year before he became Prime Minister.

Other words and phrases reveal deeper thoughts about ambition, Islam, public and private morals, jour-nalism, blood sports, climate change, the old and the young. Not forgetting Europe; lots of Europe. Very little on economics. Some of his views have stayed the same;

with others he has done a handbrake turn worthy of one of his car reviews.

The same Boris who, soon after becoming Prime Minister, told a sceptical senior banker that his economic strategy is based on 'boosterism' scoffed at another fresh new Prime Minister for taking the same approach in 1997. The 'understated, tongue-tied self-effacement' of boring John Major was what foreigners loved most about Britain, wrote Johnson, not flashy Tony Blair's 'loutish boosterism'.

The animal rights crusader who howled in 2018 that you would have to be 'crapulous' (sickeningly drunk) to fail to protest about Japanese whaling – doubtless earning the approval of partner Carrie Symonds, who works for environmental organisation Oceana – eulogised the 'gralloching' (disembowelling) of a stag a decade earlier. The man who now says he will ban the sale of new petrol and diesel cars to curb the risk of climate change flooding lampooned 'eco-warriors' in 2000 for suggesting vehicle emissions were – as he put it – 'turning the outskirts of Taunton into the Brahmaputra delta [the Bangladesh flood zone]'.

He spent most of the 2019 election campaign promising that allowing a bigger private sector stake in the NHS would 'not be on the table' in trade talks with the US. But back in 2001, he railed that the 'statist' NHS was 'the last home of socialist medicine' and treated patients like 'dolts and serfs'. Even 'tattooed bottoms' and 'the parable of the toast' (his frustration at being unable to buy a slice of toast on a hospital visit to wife Marina) were used to justify pumping more private money into the NHS.

Johnson's resounding general election victory showed that far from being intimidated or put off by his exotic, obscure (and at times contradictory) language, much of the British public felt exactly the opposite. Voters, in particular those without his privileged upbringing and educational background, were drawn to him: amused, or inspired, even.

Johnson can recite entire Shakespearean sonnets and has observed that the Bard coined 2,500 words – even more than Boris himself. He maintains that a key part of Shakespeare's appeal to the regular people who queued up to see his plays in the 1500s was that they were not 'deracinated': they reflected the politics and social culture of the day.

Shakespeare's *Henry V*, wrote Johnson, was one of the most 'rip-roaringly jingoist plays ever written', in which England was 'a place apart, a precious stone set in a silver sea … harking back to Agincourt'.

Johnson mobilised his own army of words to persuade ordinary men and women to pull off two famous victories: Brexit and the general election in 2019. Handed down from Cicero via Churchill – with a touch of Wodehouse – there is nothing deracinated about his rhetoric.

He is the Bard's patriotic Prince Hal and flatulent, fornicating Falstaff rolled into one. Without the right words, even he might vanish from the stage.

A

Acculturated

'When is Little Britain *going to do a sketch starring Matt Lucas as one of the virgins? Islam will only be truly accul-turated to our way of life when you can expect a Bradford audience to roll in the aisles at Monty Python's Life of Mohammed.'*

Daily Telegraph, 21 July 2005.

- *verb* to acculturate; to assimilate to a different culture, typically the dominant one
- see also **burqa, Kulturkampf, Little Britons, piss against the wall, raisins, re-Britannification, verkrampte, xenophobe**

Acnoid

'*I was never one of those acnoid Tory boys who had semi-erotic dreams about Margaret Thatcher.*'

Daily Telegraph, 4 May 2009.

On the devotion inspired by former Prime Minister Margaret Thatcher.

- Borisism

1

- *adjective* play on the word 'acne', the skin condition that affects teenagers
- see also **Ambrosia, Caligula dream, defenestrating, execration, flinty, matricide**

Adoptocrats

'They were considered by the system to be towards the upper limit of the age range, but there was some sympathy ... in the chilly hearts of the adoptocrats.'

Seventy-Two Virgins, 2004.

- Borisism
- *noun* morphing of 'adoption' and 'bureaucrats', officials in charge of deciding which parents can adopt children; from Latin *ad optio* 'to choose', from Greek *kratos* 'power'
- see also **quangocrat**

Aegyptia coniunx

'All three of them huff and puff about the indignity and shame of Antony's dalliance with an "Aegyptia coniunx", an Egyptian wife, in Virgil's phrase.'

The Dream of Rome, 2006.

Describing Virgil and his peers' disapproval of the love affair between Mark Antony (83 BC–30 BC), one of Julius Caesar's generals, and Queen Cleopatra of Egypt.

- *noun* from Latin *coniunx* 'wife', *aegpytia* 'Egyptian'
- see also **Burton–Taylor smooching, ceaseless carnal activity, lurve, mimetic genius, nec tali auxilio, nec defensoribus istis, soi-disant poet**

Aeneas MacTavish
'There was a time in the nineteenth century when some Scotsmen were called Aeneas, their parents under the illusion it was the same as Angus. It was bad luck on anyone christened Aeneas MacTavish – and hardly convincing.'
The Dream of Rome, 2006.
On the Victorian-era fad for Greco-Roman names. Aeneas was a Trojan hero who appears in Homer's *Iliad* and in Virgil's *Aeneid*.

- Borisism
- see also **monomaniacal, Sassenach, scandal in the wind**

Aeschylus
'Jeremy, I sit at your feet, in terms of writing about cars anyway. I'm … Aeschylus feasting from scraps from the rich banquet of Homer.'
Top Gear, 2003.
To Jeremy Clarkson, presenter of the TV motoring show.

- Borisism
- From Greek 'Aeschylus', founding father of Greek tragedy
- see also **Homeric code, nostos, scandal in the wind**

Aire fe Mabda'ak
'"Aire fe Mabda'ak," he said.'
Seventy-Two Virgins, 2004.
Arabic insult meaning 'my cock in your principles'.

- see also **acculturated, Bizzaz immak ala amood, pathetic Islamo-fascists**

3

Akratic

'Maybe he wasn't a genuine akratic. Maybe it would be more accurate to say he had a thanatos urge.'

Seventy-Two Virgins, 2004.

- *adjective* acting against one's better judgement; from Greek *akrates* 'powerless', *Thanatos*, the death instinct, personification of death in Greek mythology
- see also **gift of death**

Ambrosia

'On Mount Olympus dining on nectar and Ambrosia Creamed Rice listening to the Rolling Stones in the company of Willy Wonka, Geena Davis, Rasputin, Boudica and Margaret Thatcher.'

2000.

Describing the perfect way to spend the Millennium New Year's Eve.

- Borisism
- *noun* Ambrosia Creamed Rice, creamy tinned dessert; a play on the mythological depiction of ambrosia being the food or drink of the Greek gods
- see also **acnoid, flinty, hypothalamus, Inca mummy, Oompaloompas, sclerotic**

Anaphora

'It is a classic descending tricolon with anaphora, or repetition of key words.'

The Churchill Factor, 2014.

4

Explaining the rhetorical ploy in Churchill's tribute to RAF pilots in the 1940 Battle of Britain: 'Never ... was so much owed by so many to so few.'

- From Greek *anaphora* 'carrying back', repeating a word or phrase for artistic effect
- see also **chiasmus, dash of Dawson, numen, orotund, praeteritio, syllogism, transmogrifying, Zeus and Polyhymnia, zingers**

Antepartum

'When I look into the eyes of my seven-week-old daughter, Lara Lettice, the injustice almost chokes me up ... my daughter is a Belgian ... it did not occur to me, antepartum, that the issue of two free born British citizens could be foreign.'

The Spectator, 31 July 1993.

- *adjective* before birth; the opposite of antenatal; Latin *ante* 'before', *partum* 'giving birth'
- see also **Bwussels, fungible**

Anti-aphrodisiacal

"It's Time For Hague", proclaimed the T-shirt. As a piece of nightwear, his wife claimed it had anti-aphrodisiacal properties of a barely credible order.'

Seventy-Two Virgins, 2004.

On William Hague, Conservative leader 1997–2001.

- *noun* sexual turn-off; from Greek 'Aphrodite', Greek goddess of love
- see also **dolichocephalic, flaccidity, hippopotomonstrosequippedaliophobia, non-turgor factor, one-eyed trouser snake, phallocratic, post-coital detumescence, sexist fronde**

Araminta

'For a brief moment that car made me vaguely interesting to these gorgeous eighteen-year-olds wearing low-cut ball-gowns with names like Georgina and Araminta.'

Life in the Fast Lane, 2007.

On driving a Jaguar.

- Araminta is a hybrid of Aminta, from Greek *amyntor* 'protector and defender', and Arabella, from Latin *orabilis* 'yielding to prayer'
- see also **Boobtropolis, buxom as all get out, lolling rakes, Maenads, mega-titted, onanistic, star-struck booby, two-seater chickwagon**

Archaiser

'We've all heard of Blair the Moderniser … But there is another character: we might call him Ur-Blair. This is Ur-Blair the Archaiser.'

The Spectator, 29 April 1995.

On Tony Blair's lack of beliefs.

- *noun* one who tries to give something the appearance of being old and wise; from Greek *archaizen* 'to imitate the language of ancient authors', *ur-* from German 'first', 'original'
- see also **pretzel-words, schlockiest bonkbuster, superannuated taramasalata, tenax proposti, timorousness, vanilla nothingness, whiffled**

Aryan bull pig

'You can call me an Armenian chicken farmer or an Aryan bull pig, but don't call me incompetent.'

Response to student magazine attack on his bid to be President of the Oxford Union, 1982.

Johnson's family has roots in Turkey, which included Armenia when it was part of the Ottoman Empire. The magazine also said he was a 'pig, the victim of a hideous Nazi war experiment'.

- see also **auto-flagellation**, **Buller**, **Johnny Turk**, **Johnson-oglus**, **stooge**, **xenophobe**

Asphodel and mallow

'The point of work is not to add to Gordon Brown's tithe barn but to have the time and freedom to bunk off, read a book, play with the children ... In the words of Hesiod they know not what blessedness there is in mallow-grass and asphodel. I doubt these Puritans would even know what asphodel was.'

Have I Got Views For You, 2006.

Attacking Gordon Brown's style as Chancellor.

- *noun(s)* asphodel, from Greek *asphodelos*, a lily; from Greek mythology, an everlasting flower in the Elysian fields. Mallow, from Latin *malva*, a flower with mauve petals, historically known as an aphrodisiac, used in fertility rites. The colour mauve comes from the French name for the plant. Hesiod, seventh-century BC poet
- see also **anti-aphrodisiacal**, **filching**, **gelatinous**, **Gordonomics**, **trud**

Augean

'As we started to appreciate the Augean scale of the task we went into a kind of frenzy, shovelling and chucking all afternoon until the straw and dung and the long-forgotten corpses of ducklings flew over our heads in a blur.'

Sunday Telegraph, 19 February 2006.

On cleaning out the duck shed on his grandfather's farm as a boy.

- *adjective* from Greek mythology; in Homer's *Iliad*, King Augeas's stable of 3,000 oxen were not cleaned for thirty years, until Hercules diverted the river Alpheus through them

- see also **Aeneas MacTavish**, **Eurydice**, **Homeric code**, **nostos**

Autarkic

'Brexit is not about shutting ourselves off; it's about going global. It's not about returning to some autarkic 1950s menu of spam and cabbage and liver.'

Speech at the Policy Exchange, London, 14 February 2018.

Assuring the public that Brexit would not turn the clock back to 1950s Britain and post-war rationing.

- *adjective* the political ideal of economic self-sufficiency, from the Greek *autos* meaning 'self' and *arkein* meaning 'to rule'

- see also **backstop-ectomy**, **bottled Brexit**, **Bre-entry**, **Brexchosis**, **go whistle**, **lachrymose**, **murrain**, **raw prawn**, **whinge-o-rama**

Auto-flagellation

'It was Gladstone's habit to bellow about the abominable and bestial lust of the Turks, before going off to rescue

fallen women, and then make up for his naughty feelings with a spot of auto-flagellation.'

The Dream of Rome, 2006.

Discussing William Gladstone, nineteenth-century British Prime Minister.

- *noun* from Latin *flagellum* 'whip'; excessive self-criticism
- see also **consecrated**, **engine of Onan**, **gibbering rictus**

Axial

'The press can in no way be blamed for the axial moment of Mr Major's prime ministership, when the pound crashed out of the Exchange Rate Mechanism.'

1995.

Discussing 'Black Wednesday', 16 September 1992, when sterling crashed out of the European Exchange Rate Mechanism, an event from which John Major's premiership never recovered.

- *adjective* relating to or forming an axis
- see also **buttock exposure**, **fungible**, **platitudinous Pooters**

B

Backstop-ectomy

'It is time to have a total backstop-ectomy. Then we can make progress...'

TV interview, 20 August 2019.

Calling for the surgical removal of the so-called 'Northern Ireland backstop' clause in Brexit talks with EU leaders.

- Borisism
- *noun* to take a metaphorical surgeon's knife to the backstop
- see also **autarkic, bottled Brexit, Bre-entry, Brexchosis, go whistle, muff it, popty-ping, Scylla and Charybdis, Tantalus, whey**

Bag of ferrets

'There is something about the very marque, Alfa, that makes the seminal vesicles writhe like a bag of ferrets.'

Life in the Fast Lane, 2007.

On driving an Alfa Romeo.

- Borisism
- see also **bra-fetishist, donger, Dorking Rugby Club's second XV,**

endocrine orchestra, stung in the bum, tinplate testosterone, two-seater chickwagon, upper epidermis of the gonad

Banana-booted demigod

'They look at David Beckham … and think, what's the point of all this education? They think they can have Posh and the Porsche and the swish pad in Cheshire. They can't unless they happen to be the one in ten million who has the gifts of the banana-booted demigod.'

29 March 2007.

Tackling low education standards of young white men.

- Borisism
- England football player David Beckham was known for his 'banana shot', bending the ball in flight; his wife Victoria Beckham was 'Posh Spice' in the Spice Girls pop group
- see also **Bothamesque, midfield playmaker, namby-pamby, panther, sjambok**

Bee Gees

'In Sicily … you can see the marvellous gold-haloed mosaics of Christ Pantocrator, looking exactly like Barry Gibb of the Bee Gees.'

The Dream of Rome, 2006.

Commenting on the influence of Byzantine civilisation on Europe in the Middle Ages. 'Pantocrator' is the traditional Byzantine portrayal of Christ, meaning almighty or all-powerful.

- Borisism

- 1970s pop group the Bee Gees comprised Barry Gibb (recognisable by his long, brushed-back hair) and his brothers, Robin and Maurice
- see also **give 3Ps a chance, hypothalamus, Inca mummy**

Best of all worlds

'All is for the best in the best of all possible worlds.'
The Times, 15 November 2004.

Putting on a brave face when challenged over his dismissal for lying about his affair with Petronella Wyatt. They are the words of Dr Pangloss, the excessive optimist in Voltaire's novel *Candide*.

- *idiom* the current situation is the best one possible; Pangloss, from Greek *pan* 'all', *glossa* 'tongue'
- see also **inverted pyramid of piffle, ker-splonked, snooks**

Bibble-babble

'An enraged Brugeiste said [I] had lost all credibility as a Euro-sceptic ... Let me try to silence the vain bibble-babble of him and his kind.'
Friends, Voters, Countrymen, 2001.

Responding to claims that his praise for Michael Heseltine, his pro-EU predecessor as MP for Henley, meant he had softened his views on Europe.

- *noun* bibble, 'drink noisily', from Latin *bibere* 'to drink'; babble, 'baby talk', from Latin *babulus* 'babbler'; Margaret Thatcher's speech in Bruges, Belgium in 1988, attacking the EU, is seen as the start of Tory Euroscepticism
- see also **boss-eyed, foam-flecked hysteria, jabberama**

Biggest creep in history

'Emperor Nero was one of the biggest creeps in history.'

The Dream of Rome, 2006.

Roman Emperor Nero (37 AD–68 AD) was known for his debaucheries, political murders, persecution of Christians and the love of music that led to the probably apocryphal story that he 'fiddled' while Rome burned in the great fire of 64 AD.

- Borisism
- See also **Neronian**

Big girl's blouse

'Call an election, you great big girl's blouse.'

House of Commons, 4 September 2019.

Taunting Labour leader Jeremy Corbyn for not backing an early election.

- *noun* insult implying weakness, effeminacy
- see also **Caracas, Heisenberg, ignoratio elenchi, lachrymose, mutton-headed old mugwump, pushmi-pullyu, vole-trousered**

Bit of black

'A Midlands businessman cruising … in search, as he put it, of "a bit of black" … his eyes like an unblinking snake, past pairs of white girls in socks, shivering on corners, until he found what he wanted. Was it a burst condom, that triumph of nature over artifice, or did Dean's father pay some trifling bonus for unprotected sex?'

Seventy-Two Virgins, 2004.

- *noun* racist term, a black prostitute
- see also **half-caste**, **Hottentot**, **poule de luxe**, **sharmoota**, **watermelon smiles**

Bituminous

'He looked at the happy brown river, winking beneath the bituminous scum.'

Seventy-Two Virgins, 2004.

- *adjective* containing, or of the nature of, bitumen, a black tar-like substance used in road construction

Bizzaz immak ala amood

'Bizzaz immak ala amood.'

Seventy-Two Virgins, 2004.

Arabic insult meaning 'your mother's tits are on a pole'.

- see also **acculturated**, **aire fe mabda'ak**, **tits in a wringer**

Black abyss

'I wake up. I sit there, bolt upright, sweating and pop-eyed and trying to pray. In that dark night, you stare into the black abyss of middle age. Your body is settling into a genetically programmed pattern of decay.'

Life in the Fast Lane, 2007.

On getting older.

- see also **dodderer**, **Morpheus**

Blubbering ninny

'That's what it's all about, politics. If you dish it out, you've

got to take it, you great blubbering ninny. If they go to the trouble of hailing you in the street as a c***, it is, surely, a sign that you have arrived.'

Friends, Voters, Countrymen, 2001.

- *noun* weak person, fool who blubbers or cries when criticised; ninny, from sixteenth century, possibly shortened from 'ninny-hammer': 'ninny' and 'hammerhead'; hammer: blockhead, stupid
- see also **buttock-headed**, **jabberama**, **queynte**, **Tory tosser**, **Twitter-borne transphobes**, **vaginal endearment**

Boobtropolis

'He clicked again in irritation, and a square popped up on his screen. He saw, too late, that it was headlined "Put your nipple in my HOT mouth". Soon he found that he was in a place called Boobtropolis, or Titty City, not, frankly, that he really cared.'

Seventy-Two Virgins, 2004.

- Borisism
- *noun* city dominated by, or perhaps constructed of, big-breasted women
- see also **buxom as all get out**, **engine of Onan**, **mega-titted**, **multiple-bosomed**, **onanist**, **soutien-gorges**, **tits in a wringer**

Boondoggle

'It is known to the politico-journalistic class as a junket, jolly, freebie or boondoggle; and which is classified, for the benefit of irritable taxpayers, as a conference.'

Daily Telegraph, 11 March 2004.

On an Anglo-Italian conference in Venice attended by politicians and journalists.

- *noun* wasteful or fraudulent project; contemptuous term originating in 1930s America
- see also **glow-worm transience, nel mezzo del cammin di nostra vita, swankpot journalists**

Boosterism

'Boosterism!'

Daily Mail, 30 July 2019.

When asked to explain what his economic policy was, this was his reply.

- Borisism
- *noun* the act of putting 'rocket boosters' under the economy. Phrase originating in the pioneering days of 1800s America when remote towns talked up their prospects to attract visitors and railway financers etc. Coined by US politician J. Proctor Knott to lampoon the phenomenon
- see also **buttock exposure, cyclotron, gloomadon-poppers, gloomsters, umbilicus**

Bosky

'Churchill and Clementine passed all sorts of bowery corners and bosky nooks of a kind that might have been specifically designed to prompt a marriage proposal.'

The Churchill Factor, 2014.

On Winston Churchill's romantic pursuit of future wife Clementine.

- *adjective* covered by trees or bushes; wooded; from Middle English *bosk* 'bush'
- see also **lurve, megalopsychia, Zeus and Polyhymnia**

Boss-eyed, foam-flecked hysteria

'I can hardly condemn UKIP as a bunch of boss-eyed, foam-flecked euro hysterics, when I have been sometimes not far short of boss-eyed, foam-flecked hysteria myself.'

Speaking in 2004.

- *noun* demeaning term for wildly enthusiastic Brexit supporters; common criticism of UKIP leader Nigel Farage. Boss-eyed: origin unknown, someone with a squint or who has a damaged eye. Possible meaning of foam-flecked: being affected by opinions with more froth than facts
- see also **bottled Brexit, buzzard squint, Bwussels, fungible, give a monkey's, polish a turd, vinegarish**

Bothamesque

'I find myself performing imaginary drives, hooks and Bothamesque thuds over the bowler's head.'

Friends, Voters, Countrymen, 2001.

- Borisism
- *adjective* light-heartedly comparing his batting style in cricket to that of 1980s England cricket hero Ian Botham
- see also **banana-booted demigod, panther**

Bottled Brexit

'Theresa May is a chicken who's bottled Brexit.'

Daily Telegraph, 24 March 2019.

- *verb* to bottle it; to lose your nerve; from Cockney rhyming slang 'bottle and glass', 'arse' – to be so scared that you lose your bowel function
- see also **Brexchosis, jot and tittle, muff it, polish a turd**

Bottom pat

'Relax. It's only Kimberly, with some helpful suggestions for boosting circulation. Just pat her on the bottom and send her on her way.'

The Spectator, 17 December 2005.

Account of his laidback style as *The Spectator*'s editor, including being woken up from a nap by its publisher, Kimberly Fortier.

• see also **bottom exposure, Kylie's rear, militia amoris, pax vobiscum!, tattooed bottoms, up the Arcelor**

Bra-fetishist

'It would be considered theatrically indispensable to expose him as a cross-dresser, a bra-fetishist, alcoholic or abuser of animals ... He simply had the right stuff exploding hormonally from every orifice.'

Seventy-Two Virgins, 2004.

• *noun* someone who derives sexual excitement from bras
• see also **buxom as all get out, mega-titted, multiple-bosomed, namby-pamby, newt-fancying fetishists, soutien-gorges, spaffed**

Braggadocio

'They have no male teachers in the classroom to inspire them and interest them and, for all their braggadocio, they are, of course, lacking in intellectual confidence.'

Daily Telegraph, 12 July 2007.

On why modern young men are not good marriage prospects.

- *noun* boastfulness; Braggadochio, boastful character in Elizabethan poet Edmund Spenser's *The Faerie Queene* in 1590. He added a pseudo-Italian suffix, *occhio*, to the verb 'brag'
- see also **banana-booted demigod, chavs, feckless, Italian stallion**

Brahmaputra

'Are we all mad? cry the eco-prophets. Can we not see how vehicle emissions are turning the outskirts of Taunton into something resembling the Brahmaputra delta on a wet day … The eco-warriors' case is nonsense. There is no evidence the planet is suffering from climate change.'
Daily Telegraph, 2 November 2000.

Mocking climate change protestors.

- *noun* the Brahmaputra River is in Bangladesh's flood zone
- see also **chitterlings and chine, hempen, parenthetically, Toutatis, vertiginously**

Breaking and entering

'Yes, folks, we can all think of 101 uses for the forthcoming ID cards, not forgetting breaking and entering.'
Daily Telegraph, 25 November 2004.

On Labour plans to introduce identity cards. Pointing out that they are used by thieves to break locks.

- see also **impis, strigil**

Bre-entry

'It is important … as we make our Brexit – or Bre-entry into the world, as we should perhaps call it – to help people

to understand that a more global Britain will be a more prosperous Britain.'

House of Commons, 21 February 2017.

Promoting the UK's post-Brexit prospects.

- Borisism
- *noun* wordplay on 're-entry' and Brexit
- see also **autarkic, Brexchosis, murrain, pro having cake and eating it, punctilious, supererogatory, whey**

Bremain

'There is not a shred of idealism about the campaign to "Bremain". They are the Gerald Ratners of modern politics. The EU, they say – it's crap but we have no alternative. Well, we do and it's a glorious alternative.'

Speech in Manchester, 15 April 2016.

Attacking David Cameron's campaign to remain in the EU. In 1991 British businessman Gerald Ratner jokingly confessed that cheap products sold by his Ratners jewellery retailer were 'total crap.' It destroyed the company.

- Borisism
- *verb* to Bremain; to want Britain to remain in the EU
- see also **autarkic, Bre-entry, Brexchosis, girly swot, Hulk, toad beneath the harrow, whey, whinge-o-rama**

Brexchosis

'The only way to cure our Brexchosis is to do what we promised the people – to leave the EU, and do it properly.'

Daily Telegraph, 15 April 2019.

- Borisism
- *noun* wordplay on Brexit and *osis*, from Greek, meaning 'abnormal condition'; comparing Brexit deadlock to a paralysing medical condition
- see also **backstop-ectomy, bottled Brexit, Bre-entry, Hulk, muff it, Tantalus**

Britannia's ass

'The message is that Claudius kicked Britannia's ass.'
The Dream of Rome, 2006.

Recounting how Britannia was originally a symbol of Britain's humiliation, not strength.

- *noun* slang for backside; American version of 'arse'; from Old English *ærs*, hind part of animal
- see also **dikbil, medieval on their ass, up the Arcelor**

Broken-backed diplodocus

'The hopeless broken-backed diplodocus of a bendy bus.'
Speech at Conservative Party conference, 9 October 2012.

Mocking former Labour London Mayor Ken Livingstone's long 'bendy' buses. Johnson introduced new-style red double-deckers.

- Borisism
- *noun* from Greek *diplos* 'double' and *dokos* 'beam' after the double-beamed bones in its tail; one of the biggest dinosaurs
- see also **Châteauneuf-du-Pape cabal, newt-fancying hypocrites**

Brueghelian

'The scene, timeless, Brueghelian, of men with guns and dogs, standing by the edge of a wintry wood.'

Friends, Voters, Countrymen, 2001.

Describing a country shooting scene.

- *adjective* pastoral; Pieter Bruegel, sixteenth-century Dutch artist known for landscape and peasant scenes
- see also **gift of death, gralloched, semolina blob, sexual yipping, Tiglath-Pileser, tweed-wearing atavism**

Bufferdom

'He was a buffer, he told himself. At fifty-six he was on the threshold of bufferdom, and this was his buffer zone.'

Seventy-Two Virgins, 2004.

- Borisism
- *noun* realm of the buffer, an old, foolish (and usually conservative) man; in late Middle English, buffer also meant stammerer
- see also **buffoonery, bumbling skill, imbecilio, wise guy**

Buffoonery

'It will get easier when there is a big job to do and I can get on and do it. These points you make about image and buffoonery will fall away.'

GQ, July 2007.

Interview with Piers Morgan.

- *noun* clowning around; from Latin *buffo* 'clown'
- see also **bumbling skill, dash of Dawson, imbecilio, wise guy**

Bugger

'These days the culture of imperial Bulgaria is chiefly remembered for bequeathing the word "bugger" to the English language.'

The Dream of Rome, 2006.

Referring to the way in which the name of a tenth-century Macedonian religious sect has developed into the mild expletive used today.

- *noun, verb* interjection from medieval Latin *bulgarus* meaning 'a Bulgarian'
- see also **gigabucks, Skegness**

Buller

'Buller, buller, buller!'

Michael Cockerell's BBC TV documentary *Boris Johnson: The Irresistible Rise*, March 2013.

Boris's greeting to fellow former members of Oxford University's notorious Bullingdon Club, a private dining society noted for vandalising restaurants.

- see also **Aryan bull pig, bunkum, balderdash, tommyrot and fiddlesticks, Spheroids, stooge**

Bumbling skill

'The trick of maintaining [Britain's] influence, of course, is to go around pretending to be very bumbling ... a skill at which we excel.'

Daily Telegraph, 7 June 2012.

- *adjective* act in a confused way; from English, boom, loud noise; late Middle English, bumble, hum, drone
- see also **bufferdom, buffoonery, imbecilio, Latinate evasion, thrumming, wise guy**

Bunkum, balderdash, tommyrot and fiddlesticks

'The Civilised World must ignore idiots who tell us that ... public schools demolish all hopes most cherished for the Comprehensive System. This is twaddle, bunkum, balderdash, tommyrot, piffle and fiddlesticks of the most insidious kind.'

Eton Chronicle, 12 December 1980.

Aged sixteen, defending public schools in his school magazine.

- *noun(s)* nonsense; Bunkum, Buncombe County, North Carolina, mentioned in a speech by its congressman in 1820s to please constituents; balderdash, sixteenth-century jumble of drunks; tommyrot, from English dialect ('Tommy', fool, and 'rot'); fiddlesticks, violin fiddle sticks, from fifteenth-century English *fydylstks*, appropriated as a nonsense word
- see also **banana-booted demigod, chip-o-rama, cobblers, humbug, inverted pyramid of piffle, Spheroids**

Burqa

'It is absolutely ridiculous that people should choose to go around looking like letter boxes ... If a constituent came to my MP's surgery with her face obscured, I should feel fully

entitled ... to ask her to remove it so that I could talk to her properly. If a female student turned up at school or a university lecture looking like a bank robber then ditto...'

Daily Telegraph, 6 August 2018.

Controversially arguing that burqas are oppressive but should not be banned.

- *noun* loose garment, covering the body from head to feet, worn by some Muslim women

- see also **acculturated, re-Britannification, verkrampte, xenophobe**

Burton–Taylor smooching

'Antony and Cleopatra did some last-minute Burton–Taylor smooching before embarking on their vessels.'

The Dream of Rome, 2006.

Hollywood stars Richard Burton and Elizabeth Taylor portrayed Antony and Cleopatra in the 1963 film *Cleopatra*. The actors embarked on an affair during filming.

- *verb* to smooch; kiss or cuddle; from earlier English *smouch*

- see also **Aegyptia coniunx, ceaseless carnal activity, lurve**

Buttock exposure

'Lots of young designers specialising in buttock exposure, a few loutish Britpop stars, multi-millionaire restauranteurs who charge you £5 for a bun. After a few years of this boosterism, we will be crying out for the old [John] Majoresque understated, tongue-tied self effacement. That is the British feature foreigners prize the highest.'

Daily Telegraph, 22 October 1997.

On Tony Blair's 'Cool Britannia' campaign.

- Borisism
- See also **boosterism, buttock-headed, schlockiest bonkbuster, stonkingly rich, tank-topped bumboys, vanilla nothingness, whiffle**

Buttock-headed

'I was put off my stroke by some Luddite barracking from the Member for Glasgow Pollok. In case you can't place him, he is almost totally bald, giving him a curiously buttock-headed appearance.'

Speaking in the Commons in 2002.

Describing Ian Davidson, Labour MP for Glasgow Pollok 1997–2005.

- *adjective* term of abuse, comparing a bald pate to a bottom. Luddite, workers opposed to new technology; Ned Ludd, a weaver said to have broken two stocking frames in a fit of rage in 1779
- see also **buttock exposure, dolichocephalic, gibbering rictus, unclove**

Buxom as all get out

'It was going to be a buxom day. He grinned and thought of all the things that might be classified as buxom. Obviously there was Mrs (Nellie) Naaotwa Onyeama. She was as buxom as all get out. This he had amply confirmed just before he rose from her bed.'

Seventy-Two Virgins, 2004.

A character describing his liking for big-breasted women.

- *idiom* large-breasted
- see also **Boobtropolis, lascivious matrons, mega-titted,**

multiple-bosomed, soutien-gorges, two-seater chickwagon, wenching

Buzzard squint

'Whenever George Dubya Bush appears on television, with his buzzard squint and his Ronald Reagan side-nod, I find a cheer rising irresistibly in my throat. Yo, Bush baby ... tell all those pointy headed liberals where to get off.'

Daily Telegraph, 5 April 2001.

Defending US President George W. Bush.

- Borisism
- buzzard, a bird of prey; Bush's squint was satirised by American comedians such as Will Ferrell
- see also **boss-eyed, dada-ist, foam-flecked hysteria, monochrome Manichean, orally extemporising, stupefying ignorance**

Bwussels

'If we left the EU, we would have to recognise that most of our problems are not caused by "Bwussels", but by chronic British short-termism, inadequate management, sloth, low skills...'

Daily Telegraph, 12 May 2013.

On the pros and cons of leaving the EU.

- Borisism
- mocking term for Brussels, where the headquarters of the EU are located
- see also **antepartum, bibble-babble, feckless, fungible, give a monkey's, vinegarish**

C

Cachinnate

'For three whole minutes [Churchill] stands there, while the Tories cachinnate, and the opposition benches try to make noises of sympathy … This is a disaster, a living death…'
The Churchill Factor, 2014.

Conservative MPs laughed at Churchill, while opposition MPs supported him, when he dried up due to a brain malfunction during a passionate speech in support of workers' rights in 1904.

- *verb* to cachinnate; to roar with laughter, from Latin *cachinnare* 'to laugh loudly'
- see also **anaphora, chiasmus, epiphenomena, megalopsychia, orotund, runty kid, syllogism, Zeus and Polyhymnia, zingers**

Caligula gleam

'His eyes flashed with something like the Caligula gleam of our lamented Leaderene … One day … this demi-god will complete his imitation of Thatcher. He will be turfed out with tears and ignominy.'
Daily Telegraph, 30 September 1998.

On Tony Blair's Labour conference speech.

- Borisism
- Roman Emperor Caligula (12 AD–41 AD), famed for madness, brutality, incest, feeding prisoners to wild beasts and trying to appoint his horse as a consul; French President François Mitterrand said Margaret Thatcher had the 'eyes of Caligula and mouth of Marilyn Monroe'
- see also **Führerprinzip**, **matricide**, **pater patriae**

Camp Plantagenets

'There were camp Plantagenets with tilted necks and two fingers raised in benediction, or they would be raised in benediction if they had survived a century and a half of sulphur and pigeon dung.'

Seventy-Two Virgins, 2004.

Describing sculptures of Plantagenet kings in Westminster Hall.

- Borisism
- *noun* the French House of Plantagenet ruled England and parts of France from the twelfth to the fifteenth centuries; Boris's 'camp Plantaganets' is a facetious description of the pose of the sculptures with an outstretched hand
- see also **consecrated**, **Taliban chappies**, **tank-topped bumboys**, **up the Arcelor**

Cannae

'It was the Tory party's Cannae.'

Friends, Voters, Countrymen, 2001.

On the iconic defeat of Conservative Cabinet minister Michael Portillo in the 1997 election.

- The Battle of Cannae, 216 BC, was one of the Roman Army's worst defeats; up to 80,000 Roman soldiers were slaughtered by Hannibal's Carthaginians
- see also **pudding basin**, **Pyrrhic**, **supercilious sibilance**

Caracas

'Jeremy Corbyn's response to the grisly events in Venezuela is to side with the regime … He says he still admires Bolivarian revolutionary socialism. I say he's Caracas.'
Speech at Conservative Party conference, 3 October 2017.

Substituting the term 'crackers' for Caracas, the capital of Venezuela.

- Borisism
- see also **big girl's blouse**, **Heisenberg**, **hempen**, **ignoratio elenchi**, **lachrymose**, **pushmi-pullyu**, **vole-trousered**

Caramelised

'When he came to describe the fate of the Iraqis, how they were first caramelised, then carbonised, and how their molten fat ran in rivulets down the sides of their incinerated car seats…'
Seventy-Two Virgins, 2004.

A character describing victims of a car bomb.

- *verb* cooking term when sugar is mixed with alcohol and set alight; melting and caramelising; from Latin *calamellus* 'little reed', probably referring to sugar cane
- see also **cauls**

Caseomaniac

"'Or try this one, my dear sir," the caseomaniac would say.'
Seventy-Two Virgins, 2004.

- Borism
- *noun* describing a fellow cheese lover; from Latin *caseus* 'cheese', from Proto-Indo-European root *kwat* 'to ferment', 'become sour'
- see also **chitterlings and chine, cruelty of veganism**

Casus belli

'What makes me angry is that Blair concentrated on this casus belli *– WMD – when some of us argued for ages that it was nonsense.'*
Speaking in 2004.

Calling for Tony Blair to be impeached over the Iraq War.

- *noun* from Latin *casus belli* 'occasion of war'; an act or situation that provokes or justifies war
- see also **Archaiser, gelatinous, pretzel-words, schlockiest bonk-buster, superannuated taramasalata, turnip ghost, whiffled**

Cauls

'The bluish organs with their white cauls of fat, the long pulsing pipes, everything folded and fitted to some mysterious pattern. Surely there was a maker at work here.'
Life in the Fast Lane, 2007.

Describing the culmination of a stag hunt, seeing a higher meaning in the end result.

- *noun* amniotic membrane enclosing a foetus

- see also **caramelised, gift of death, gralloched, semolina blob, sexual yipping, Tiglath-Pileser, tweed-wearing atavism**

Ceaseless carnal activity

'By 34 BC, it was felt that Antony's brain had been softened by ceaseless carnal activity.'

The Dream of Rome, 2006.

On Antony and Cleopatra.

- *noun* non-stop sex; from Latin *carnalis* 'of the flesh'
- see also **Burton–Taylor smooching, lurve, mother-bonking, one-eyed trouser snake, wenching**

Charismatic megafauna

'I felt the surge of excitement that I imagine you must get on safari, when after days of scanning the veld you finally see … some species of charismatic megafauna … the noble curve of the brow, like a bowler hat or an African elephant.'

Daily Telegraph, 19 March 2012.

Seeing London's new double-decker buses.

- *noun* large animals like pandas and elephants with symbolic value or popular appeal; from Greek *mega* 'great'; from Latin 'Faunus', god of the forest, plain and fields
- see also **broken-backed diplodocus, Brueghelian, Hyrcanian tiger, impis, taxidermy, Tsavo, tweed-wearing atavism**

Châteauneuf-du-Pape cabal

'We fought to keep London from lurching back into the grip of a Marxist cabal of taxpayer-funded

Châteauneuf-du-Pape-swilling tax minimisers and bendy-bus fetishists.'

Speech at Conservative Party conference, 9 October 2012.

When he became the Mayor of London Boris claimed to have found over 100 bottles of the vintage red wine in a 'secret cellar', left by his Labour predecessor Ken Livingstone.

- *noun* secret political clique of left-wing hypocrites; from Kabbalah, meaning 'reception' or 'tradition', the Jewish mystical interpretation of Hebrew scripture. By the seventeenth century it came to mean a secretive political group. The theory that it stems from the CABAL initials of King Charles II's five ministers who signed a secret treaty with France is a folk myth, but may have popularised its usage
- see also **bra-fetishists, broken-backed diplodocus, hogwhimpering, newt-fancying hypocrites**

Chavs

'The real divide is between the entire class of people now reposing their fat behinds on the green and red benches in the Palace of Westminster, and the bottom twenty per cent of society – the group that supplies us with the chavs, the losers, the burglars, the drug addicts...'

Daily Telegraph, 1995.

- *noun* pejorative slang for anti-social lower-class youth in sportswear; probably from Romany *chavo* 'boy, youth' or *chavvy* 'baby, child'
- see also **banana-booted demi-god, feckless, nephos, pikeys**

Chiasmus

'When he uncorks this one at the Lord Mayor's Banquet, you hear his audience laugh with pleasure and surprise. That is because ... it is varied by chiasmus, in that he swaps "beginning" and "end".'

The Churchill Factor, 2014.

Analysing Churchill's rhetorical technique during his speech after the Battle of El Alamein: 'This is not the end. It is not even the beginning of the end. But it is, perhaps, the end of the beginning.'

- *noun* rhetorical device from Ancient Greece and Rome in which words or concepts are repeated in reverse order for greater effect; from Latin via Greek *chiázō* 'shape like the letter X', a crossing or reversal

- see also **anaphora, orotund, syllogism, Zeus and Polyhymnia**

Chip-o-rama

'Stop this chip-o-rama rubbish!'

House of Commons, 15 March 2007.

Brushing off a Labour MP's complaint that there are too many Eton students at top universities.

- Borisism
- *noun* based on proverb 'having a chip on one's shoulder' – a grudge or sense of entitlement. In nineteenth-century North America, when two young men were in dispute, a chip of wood would be placed on the shoulder of one and the other would try to knock it off
- **bunkum, balderdash, tommyrot and fiddlesticks, Spheroids**

Chitterlings and chine

'We are going to have carnivorous festivals of chops and sausages and burgers and chitterlings and chine and offal and the fat will run down our chins.'

Daily Telegraph, 9 September 2008.

Defiant response to calls to reduce meat eating.

- Borisism
- *noun* chitterlings, small intestine of a pig; chine, backbone of an animal
- see also **caseomaniac, cruelty of veganism, dikbil, toxoplasmosis**

Chunderous

'Even Hezza, who might have been pleased, seems to think it chunderous.'

Friends, Voters, Countrymen, 2001.

Describing Michael Heseltine's reaction to Boris's observation that succeeding him as MP for Henley was like Simba the cub following his father Mufasa, King of the Pride, in Disney's *The Lion King*.

- *adjective* nauseating, revolting; chunder, Australian slang for vomit. Sailors about to vomit out of a porthole are said to have shouted 'watch under' to prevent those in lower cabins being sprayed with sick, although this could be folklore
- see also **defenestrating, Jackson Pollocked, pharaonic Hezzapolis, sac de vomissement, Simba, stumblebum, ululations**

Cincinnatus

'Were I to be pulled like Cincinnatus from my plough, then obviously it would be a great privilege.'

Mail on Sunday, 23 August 2008.

Response to author on being asked if he would like to succeed David Cameron as Prime Minister.

- Cincinnatus (c. 519 BC–c. 430 BC) was a Roman statesman and general of legendary virtue who came out of retirement on his farm in 458 BC to save Rome from attack – and then returned to tilling the soil

- see also **cursus honorum, Disraeli and Achilles, Eurydice, girly swot, pater patriae, reincarnated as an olive, world king**

Cleggster

'Never mind the badgers – save the Cleggster from extermination!'

Daily Telegraph, 24 September 2012.

Tongue-in-cheek defence of Lib Dem leader Nick Clegg, David Cameron's coalition government partner, when Clegg's ratings plummeted.

- see also **inanition, taxidermy, yellow albatross**

Clinkie

'Whenever we go to India, we have to bring "clinkie" in our luggage ... There is a duty of 150 per cent in India on imports of Scotch whisky. So we have to bring it in duty-free for our relatives.'

Speaking at a Sikh temple in Bristol, May 2017.

Boris was criticised by some for making this remark at a temple. The Sikh religion bans alcohol.

- Borisism
- *noun* slang for bottle; the sound of clinking bottles in luggage
- see also **crapulous, hogwhimpering**

Cobblers

'*The CIA had expressly warned the British government that the forty-five minute claim was a load of old cobblers.*'
Daily Telegraph, 29 April 2004.

On Tony Blair's claim that Saddam Hussein had weapons of mass destruction and could fire them at British targets within forty-five minutes.

- *idiom* coarse slang, mild insult meaning nonsense; from Cockney rhyming slang for testicles ('balls') based on 'cobbler's awls'; awls are the pointed hand tools that cobblers (shoe menders) used to punch holes in leather
- see also **Archaiser, casus belli, gonad, pretzel-words, schlockiest bonkbuster, Spheroids, superannuated taramasalata**

Coddle

'*After some hours coddling my brain…*'
Friends, Voters, Countrymen, 2001.

- *verb* to coddle; cook in water below boiling point; used here as a metaphor for 'racking' one's brain; from Latin *calidus* 'warm'
- see also **stooge**

Coelacanth

'He's a political coelacanth. A fossil. He's been dredged up in the nets of some super-trawler from the Mariana Trench of politics.'

The Sun, 3 November 2019.

Describing Jeremy Corbyn.

- Borisism
- *noun* fish thought to have become extinct in the dinosaur age until it was rediscovered in the 1930s; the Mariana Trench is the planet's deepest point, located in the western Pacific Ocean
- see also **hempen**, **mutton-headed old mugwump**

Condom stuffed with walnuts

'If Arnold Schwarzenegger looks like a condom stuffed with walnuts, the Delfino is like a bin liner containing a couple of televisions.'

Life in the Fast Lane, 2007.

On driving a Delfino sports car.

- Borisism
- see also **monosyllabic Austrian cyborg**, **pink-eyed terminators**

Consecrated

'If gay marriage was OK – and I was uncertain on the issue – then I saw no reason in principle why a union should not be consecrated between three men, as well as two men, or indeed three men and a dog.'

Friends, Voters, Countrymen, 2001.

Comparing gay marriage to bestiality.

- *verb* made sacred, from Latin *sacrare* 'to declare sacred, sanctify, immortalise'
- see also **auto-flagellation, camp plantagenets, sexist fronde, Taliban chappies, tank-topped bumboys, up the Arcelor**

Coon

'"You stupid little... coon!" ... There it was, en clair, decoded. He was a coon, and he was stupid, and he was stupid because he was a coon ... "Stupid little coon," he said to himself, as though reciting a passage from the Koran.'

Seventy-Two Virgins, 2004.

- *noun* racist derogatory term for a black person; from 'raccoon' via Native American Powhatan *arocoun*
- see also **half-caste, Hottentot, puffing coolies, sexist fronde, watermelon smiles**

Cornflakes

'The income gap between the top cornflakes and bottom cornflakes is wider than ever. Too many cornflakes aren't being given a good enough chance to rustle and hustle their way to the top.'

Speech at the Centre for Policy Studies think tank, November 2013.

Talking about social mobility.

- see also **Octavian the cornflake, Ready Brek glow**

Crack-brained neocons

'None of the crack-brained neocons had really been confronted with the full awfulness of their doctrines.'

Seventy-Two Virgins, 2004.

- *noun* foolish, crazy; from Greek *neos* 'new', and from Latin *conservativus* 'to conserve'
- 1960s American term to describe right-wing conservatives who believed the US should use its military power to settle other countries' problems, such as George W. Bush's 2003 Iraq War
- see also **buzzard squint**, **dada-ist**, **monochrome Manichean**, **Stilton-eating surrender monkeys**, **stupefying ignorance**

Crapshoot

'I forgot that to rely on a train, in Blair's Britain, is to engage in a crapshoot with the devil.'

Daily Telegraph, 3 July 2003.

On a train delay that caused him to miss a TV appearance.

- *noun* gamble; craps, an American game where players bet on the roll of a dice
- see also **Archaiser**, **pretzel-words**, **raging homunculus**, **whiffled**

Crapulous

'Are we so bleared and crapulous with the effects of Christmas that we have failed to take it in?'

Daily Telegraph, 30 December 2018.

Criticising the lack of outrage over Japan resuming commercial whaling.

- *adjective* sickness caused by too much alcohol; from Latin *crapulosus* 'inclined to excess drinking'
- see also **Brueghelian**, **cauls**, **gift of death**, **gralloched**

Cruelty of veganism

'I did briefly experiment with veganism. It didn't last ... I think it was the sheer cruelty of being deprived of cheese.'

The Times, 9 June 2019.

- see also **caseomaniac, chitterlings and chine**

Cursus honorum

'My ambition silicon chip has been programmed to try to scramble up this cursus honorum, this ladder of things.'

Desert Island Discs, BBC Radio 4, 30 October 2005.

Being driven to get to the top in politics.

- *noun* the ascending order of public offices; from Latin, 'course of honours', known colloquially as the 'ladder of offices'
- see also **Cincinnatus, Disraeli and Achilles, reincarnated as an olive, selfish tosser, snooks, thrumming, world king**

Cyclotron

'Britain is not only the place where the atom was first split but has become a gigantic cyclotron of talent in which people are coming together from every discipline to produce constant flashes of inspiration.'

Speech at Conservative Party conference, 3 October 2017.

- *noun* a type of particle accelerator which accelerates charged particles outwards from its centre along a spiral path. Invented 1935, cyclo merged with electron
- see also **boosterism**

D

Dada-ist

'I defy anyone to watch ... [his] gaffes and bloopers without a sense of wonder at his Prescottian battles with the English language. He resembles ... a linguistic dada-ist armed with nuclear weapons and a worrying sense that God is on his side.'

Daily Telegraph, 12 January 2009.

Comparing George W. Bush to Tony Blair's foot-in-mouth Deputy Prime Minister John Prescott.

- *adjective* someone who ridicules the standards of society; Dadaism, an intellectual movement embraced by 1920s avant-garde artists who used nonsense in their works

- see also **buzzard squint, crack-brained neocons, monochrome Manichean, orally extemporising**

Daks

'On the streets of London I wore the same "Stubbies" daks – shorts of appalling brevity – I had worn in the bush until my girlfriend said it was her or the "Stubbies" daks. They were designed by an itinerant tailor, who came to take my

measurements in my glass-sided office. He made me drop
my daks in full view of the assorted Telegraph *beauties.'*
Friends, Voters, Countrymen, 2002.

- *noun* Australian slang for trousers; Daks, 1930s brand of trousers
- see also **chunderous, donger, raw prawn, witchetty grub**

Dash of Dawson

'A mixture of Pericles and Abraham Lincoln with a small
but irrefutable dash of Les Dawson.'
The Churchill Factor, 2014.

On Churchill's oratory.

- Borisism
- Leslie Dawson Jr (1931–93) was a popular English comedian famous for his deadpan style, cantankerous persona and sexist 'wife' jokes
- see also **funky Gibbon, Gibbonian, megalopsychia, runty kid, selfish tosser, transmogrifying, Zeus and Polyhymnia, zingers**

Decibelic

'The pig farmer gave a decibelic denunciation of Brussels
and its agricultural policy.'
Friends, Voters, Countrymen, 2001.

- *adjective* very loud; decibel, from Latin *decimus* 'tenth' (unit, one tenth of a bel)
- see also **dithyramb, fungible, vinegarish**

Defenestrating

'Someone suggested that my very presence on the shortlist

was another attempt at Thatcherian revenge on Tarzan, for defenestrating her in 1990.'

Friends, Voters, Countrymen, 2001.

The suggestion that his selection as Michael Heseltine's successor as Henley MP in 2001 was to avenge Margaret Thatcher's defeat at Heseltine's hands.

- *verb* to defenestrate; throw someone out of a window; removing them from power. From Latin *de* 'down from', *fenestra* 'window.' In the 1618 Defenestration of Prague three Catholic officials were thrown from the top-floor window of a castle by a mob
- see also **entasis, matricide, pharaonic Hezzapolis, Simba, ululations**

Demotic

'He was only pretending. I think he knew full well what Magna Carta means. It was a brilliant move in order to show his demotic credentials and that he didn't have Latin bursting out of every orifice.'

LBC Radio, 27 September 2012.

Facetious comment on David Cameron's gaffe on US TV show *Late Show with David Letterman* when he appeared not to know that Magna Carta stands for 'Great Charter'.

- *adjective* relating to language used by ordinary people; from Greek *demotes* 'one of the people'
- see also **girly swot, schmoozathon, toad beneath the harrow**

Deracinated

'Shakespeare's plays are not deracinated masterpieces ...

by some garret-bound egghead with a bad haircut. They derived their energy and resonance from events at the time.'

The Spirit of London, 2012.

Stating that Shakespeare was not a remote intellectual – his writing mirrored the politics and culture of his day.

- French *racine* 'root' via Latin *radix* 'root'; French *de* 'from'
- see also **lurve, Montagues and Capulets**

Descamisados

'Like Evita … she appeals to Britain's equivalent of the descamisados, *the shirtless ones. Like Evita, she was partly vulgar, with democratic tastes in rollerskating and baseball caps … an icon for homosexuals, ethnic minorities … Did she not take an Egyptian as her lover?'*

Daily Telegraph, 3 September 1997.

Thoughts on the death of Lady Diana. The *descamisados* were the poor of Argentina who idolised Evita Perón, husband of Argentinian President Juan Perón.

- Borisism
- *descamisados*, Spanish for 'shirtless'
- see also **mimetic genius, sexually liberated**

Dikbil

'On one side [of no-man's land] there are some of those famous Belgian Blanc Bleu cows, with the dikbil.'

The Churchill Factor, 2014.

Visiting a First World War battlefield in Belgium.

- *noun* the naturally large rumps of Belgian cattle that produce fine steaks; from Dutch, 'double buttock'
- see also **chitterlings and chine**, **cruelty of veganism**

Diocletian

'Possibly the most deluded measure to come from Europe since Diocletian tried to fix the price of groceries across the Roman Empire.'

The Times, March 2013.

Attacking EU plans to cap bankers' bonuses.

- Diocletian (284 AD–305 AD) prompted riots after fixing the cost of commodities
- see also **boosterism**

Diolch yn fawr

'Diolch yn fawr … I am grateful to my hon. Friend, who speaks for Wales. It is a great deal for England, Scotland, Wales and Northern Ireland.'

House of Commons, 19 October 2019.

Addressing a Welsh Conservative MP in a debate on Brexit.

- Welsh for 'thank you very much'
- see also **popty-ping**, **pysgod a sglodion**

Dirndl

'Beaming girls in dirndl serving foaming steins in the biergarten.'

The Churchill Factor, 2014.

- *noun* traditional Alpine peasant girl's costume with tight

waistband, low-cut blouse and close-fitting bodice; from south
German dialect, *dirne* 'girl'

- see also **Boobtropolis**, **buxom as all get out**, **mega-titted**

Disraeli and Achilles

*'Disraeli was once asked why people went to the Commons,
and he said, "We do it for fame." Achilles said he was doing
it all for the glory of song and immortality.'*
GQ, July 2007.
Asked by Piers Morgan if he was a celebrity.

- Benjamin Disraeli (1804–81) was twice Conservative Prime Minister between 1868 and 1880; Achilles is the hero of the Trojan War
  in Homer's epic poem *Iliad*
- see also **Aeschylus**, **Cincinnatus**, **cursus honorum**, **egotistical
  glory-mania**, **nostos**, **snooks**, **thrumming**, **world king**

Dithyramb

*'Now that I came to think of it, I did remember producing
an extended dithyramb of hate against the Common Agricultural Policy...'*
Daily Telegraph, 11 March 2004.
Joking about being excluded from a press junket organ-
ised by European leaders.

- *noun* an ancient Greek hymn, especially one dedicated to Dionysus, god of wine and fertility, sung and danced with vehemence
  and fervour; from Greek *dithurambos*
- see also **boss-eyed**, **foam-flecked hysteria**, **decibelic**, **fungible**,
  give a monkey's, **vinegarish**

Divine gift of lewdness

'The object of his lust was an eighteen-year-old actress. The great thing about Gertrude, Wilkes told a friend, was that unlike most English and French women of that epoch, she believed in taking her clothes off in bed. She was possessed of the "divine gift of lewdness."'

The Spirit of London, 2012.

On John Wilkes, rabble-rousing eighteenth-century radical, journalist and MP.

- Borisism
- see also **ceaseless carnal activity**, **ecclesiastical bunga-bunga**, **fantastic goer**, **lascivious matrons**, **lolling rakes**, **Paris Hilton**, **tinplate testosterone**

Dobby

'Despite looking a bit like Dobby the House Elf, he is a ruthless and manipulative tyrant.'

Daily Telegraph, 6 December 2015.

On Vladimir Putin.

- 'Dobby', the bald, floppy-eared, pointy-nosed, bug-eyed house elf in J. K. Rowling's *Harry Potter* books
- see also **revanchist**, **torrents of obfuscation**

Dodderer

'White-haired dodderers in their Clouseau-like kepis.'

The Churchill Factor, 2014.

Describing incompetent ageing French Second World War generals.

- *noun* one who shakes or trembles, usually with old age; from English verb, to dodder, from obsolete English dialect, *dadder* 'dither'. Kepi is a French military cap, from the Swiss German *kappe*. Inspector Clouseau, the fictional French detective in the *Pink Panther* comedy films, wore a hat
- see also **black abyss**

Doggerland

'Britain and Holland used to be joined by a territory known as Doggerland.'

Speech at the Policy Exchange think tank, 14 February 2018.

Talking up the links between Britain and Europe.

- *noun* landmass connecting Britain to continental Europe until it was flooded by rising sea levels around 6500 BC; named after the Dogger Bank, sandbank in a shallow part of the North Sea, in turn named after 'doggers', seventeeth-century Dutch fishing boats

Dolichocephalic

'If you were an ancient Athenian politician and you went bald ... you didn't have to worry the electorate would harp on about it, as they do when confronted by a bald Tory leader. Pericles was a slaphead with a dolichocephalic skull; but he had a cool solution. He wore a hoplite helmet, morning, noon and night.'

Daily Telegraph, 8 July 2004.

On bald Tory leader William Hague.

- *noun* long-headed; from Greek *dolikhos* 'long' and *kephalos* 'head'. Hoplites were citizen-soldiers of the city-states of Ancient Greece; ornate helmets were part of their armoury. Pericles (495 BC–429

BC), a Greek orator and statesman, wore one to conceal his unusually shaped head

- see also **anti-aphrodisiacal properties, buttock-headed, dash of Dawson, Pericles**

Dolts and serfs

'One of the reasons why the NHS is no longer the envy of the world is that it is still top-down, statist and treats patients like serfs and dolts. Britain is the last home of socialist medicine.'

Daily Telegraph, 14 June 2001.

Arguing that the NHS does not work because it regards patients as stupid peasants with no choice to go elsewhere for treatment.

- *noun(s)* dolt, from early English, *dulled*; serf, from Latin *servus*, 'to serve'
- see also **not on the table, parable of the toast, tattooed bottoms**

Donger

'I wouldn't be at all surprised if he's been up to some kind of beastliness again, whanging the old donger in the kedgeree I have no doubt...'

Seventy-Two Virgins, 2004.

- *noun* slang for a penis; from English 'dong', sound of a large bell. Australian saying, 'dry as a dead dingo's donger'; kedgeree, unknown sexual slang
- see also **bag of ferrets, bra-fetishist, flaccidity, non-turgor factor, one-eyed trouser snake, phallocratic phallus**

Donnez-moi un break

'My message to M van Rompuy is donnez-moi un break, mate.'

Daily Telegraph, 19 November 2012.

On EU budget rises. Despite being fluent in French, Boris has used 'Franglais' for effect.

- Borisism
- *idiom* to protest; to ask someone to stop treating you unfairly;'give me a break': thought to be from underworld term for collecting money for a convict on release from prison – 'he was given a break'. Herman Van Rompuy, President of the European Council 2009–14
- see also **ils sont passes, ces beaux jours, sac de vomissment**

Dorking Rugby Club's second XV

'Heaven knows what he thought was going on inside – Naomi Campbell being pleasured by Dorking Rugby Club's second XV, or something equally decadent.'

Life in the Fast Lane, 2007.

On being spotted lying on the rear seat of a people carrier with black tinted windows while reviewing it for *GQ* magazine.

- see also **fully extended bonk, gynaecomorphised, Italian stallion, poule de luxe, two-seater chickwagon**

Drag artistry

'Give that man a handbag ... tell him to wear a powder blue suit and a pineapple-coloured wig next time he wants to

impersonate this country's greatest peace-time prime minister. Yesterday we had a shameless piece of drag artistry.'

Daily Telegraph, 30 September 1998.

Accusing Tony Blair of copying Margaret Thatcher's 'The Lady's Not For Turning' speech.

- Borism
- *noun* performance by a man dressing and acting like a woman
- See also **Caligula gleam**, **Führerprinzip**, **phenotype**

Dramaturgy

'John Prescott's role is to be part of the dramaturgy of New Labour in which, by their lumpen cavortings, the Prime Minister's underlings intensify the apparent radiance of Tony Blair.'

Friends, Voters, Countrymen, 2001.

On Blair's Deputy Prime Minister John Prescott.

- *noun* the theory and study of dramatic composition, invented by eighteenth-century German writer Gotthold Ephraim Lessing
- see also **dada-ist**, **Führerprinzip**

DUDE

'Some wag has already pointed out that "deliver, unite and defeat" was not the perfect acronym for an election campaign, since it spells DUD. They forgot the final "E" for energise. I say to all the doubters, "Dude, we are going to energise the country."'

Victory speech upon winning the Conservative leadership, 23 July 2019.

- Borisism
- *noun* informal term for a man (or woman), often as a form of address; used here as a jokey acronym
- see also **Bre-entry**, **whey**

Dur-brained

'How dur-brained do you have to be to fail to grasp that pebble beaches are uneven and may be slippery?'
Daily Telegraph, 6 July 2009.
On health and safety laws.

- *adjective* insult, most often used by children, for someone deemed stupid; possibly variant of similar American insult, 'dough-brained'
- see also **encephalopathic**, **multiple-bosomed**, **scabophobic**

Dusky

'I suspect it is a cynical attempt to pander to the many who think the world would be a better place if dangerous folk with dusky skins were just slammed away … It is heroic of the Tories to oppose it.'
Daily Telegraph, 10 March 2005.
Opposing new anti-terror laws proposed by Tony Blair.

- *adjective* having slightly dark skin; considered to be a racist term
- see also **half-caste**, **Hottentot**, **Nilotic**, **puffing coolies**, **watermelon smiles**

Dykes

'I've got my fingers in several dykes.'
Speech at Conservative Party conference, 6 October 2004.

- *noun* flippant use of the idiom '[to have one's] finger in the dyke', emergency measures to stem the flow of something undesirable; also offensive slang for lesbian

Dystopian fantasy

'Digital authoritarianism is not, alas, the stuff of dystopian fantasy but of an emerging reality.'

Speech to the UN General Assembly in New York, 24 September 2019.

On the dangers of artificial intelligence.

- *noun* an imaginary nightmarish futuristic society; from Greek, *dys* 'bad/hard', *topia* 'place/landscape'
- see also **pullulate**

E

Ebullition

'Sometimes, after he had been brought to an ebullition of anger, he started to wonder whether he might be made of the same stuff.'

Seventy-Two Virgins, 2004.

- *noun* outburst of emotion or violence; from Latin *ebullire* 'to boil up'
- see also **get stuffed, pathetic Islamofascists**

E pluribus unum

'Here we all were trying to forge a federal state, e pluribus unum, and the Serbs and Croats were on the point of destroying federal Yugoslavia.'

Writing in 2008.

Contrasting efforts to create a federal EU with the ongoing Balkan War which was decimating the former Yugoslavia.

- *noun* from Latin, 'out of many, one', a traditional motto of the US marking its thirteen colonies uniting as one in 1776
- see also **give a monkey's, homo foederalis**

Ecclesiastical bunga-bunga

'The idiotic rites of the Medmenham Monks. Think of Silvio Berlusconi's bunga-bunga room, but with an ecclesiastical theme. High class hookers or adventurous ladies of fashion were invited to dinner at the end of which the women would choose a partner and repair to the monk's cell.'
The Spirit of London, 2012.

Comparing the eighteenth-century sexual high jinks of senior political and court figures, including radical politician John Wilkes, at Medmenham Abbey in Buckinghamshire, to Italian Prime Minister Silvio Berlusconi's 'bunga-bunga' sex parties.

- Borism
- see also **ceaseless carnal activity, divine gift of lewdness, feline prowlings, imperial good-time girls, lolling rakes, wenching**

Ecstasy of Widdecombe

'Pity us who are so unfortunate as to speak to audiences who have known the ecstasy of [Ann] Widdecombe.'
Friends, Voters, Countrymen, 2001.

Politician Ann Widdecombe, much-loved for her elephantine performances on the BBC TV show *Strictly Come Dancing* – and passionate after-dinner speeches delivered in a shriek.

- Borism
- *noun* the joy of audiences entertained by outspoken former Conservative MP Ann Widdecombe
- see also **Hottentot, rictus of amazement**

Egotistical glory-mania

'Sometimes the old guard disapproved of this egotistical glory-mania, and sometimes Rome was dragged into conflicts she did not start.'

The Dream of Rome, 2006.

- *adjective* excessively absorbed in oneself, self-centred; from Latin *ego* 'I'

- see also **Disraeli and Achilles, epic poem**

Empyrean

'He dreams of cabbage whites coming through the open kitchen window, and red kites hovering in the blue empyrean...'

Friends, Voters, Countrymen, 2001.

- *noun* relating to heaven or the sky; the highest part of heaven, thought by ancient cosmologists to be the realm of pure fire. From Greek via medieval Latin *empurios*, from *en* 'in', *pur* 'fire'

Encephalopathic

'They have taken the sword of common sense to the great bloated encephalopathic sacred cow of elf and safety. And for this effrontery they are being persecuted by the authorities. What do they want? They want their children, aged eight and five, to have the right to walk or cycle one mile to school.'

Daily Telegraph, 25 July 2010.

Defending a couple challenging a local authority ban on their children travelling to school unsupervised.

- *adjective* diseased brain; from Greek *enkephalos* 'within the head', *patheia* 'suffering'
- see also **dur-brained, multiple-bosomed, scabophobic**

Endocrine orchestra

'She was blonde. She was beautiful ... And she had just overtaken me ... I wasn't having it. If there is one thing calculated to make the testosterone slosh in your ears like the echoing sea ... it's being treated as though you were an old woman by a young woman ... The whole endocrine orchestra said: "Go. Take."'

Life in the Fast Lane, 2007.

On driving an Alfa Romeo car.

- Borisism
- *noun* the endocrine glands produce hormones; from Latin via Greek, *endon* 'inside, within', *krino* 'to separate'
- see also **bag of ferrets, gynaecomorphised, hypothalamus, Italian stallion, phallocratic phallus, tinplate testosterone**

Engine of Onan

'The internet is the engine of Onan. A glorified intercontinental wankerama. I thought I'd just tap in the word "girls" ... I was welcomed to Boobtropolis. What if someone else turned it on and found all these fantastic nude chicks still there, a-pouting and a-begging? It bellowed "Welcome to Titty City!"'

The Spectator, 22 January 2000.

Being caught by Arthur the office caretaker surfing the
internet for porn – out of curiosity.

- Borisism
- see also **Boobtropolis, jabberama, onanistic, phallocratic phallus, pullulate, spaffed, wankerer**

Entasis

*'Michael Heseltine was famous for the amazing architecture
of his suits: the hammer-beams of his shoulder pads, the
flying buttress of his lapels, the subtle entasis of his trousers.'*
Friends, Voters, Countrymen, 2001.

- *noun* a slight bulge built into the middle of classical Greek columns,
like the Parthenon, to correct an optical illusion and make them
appear straighter and taller. From Greek *enteinein* 'to stretch or strain'
- see also **chunderous, matricide, pharaonic Hezzapolis, Simba**

Epic poem

*'I want to write an epic poem about Roy. It's amazing. He
just wants everything – the fame, the power, the girls, the
good life.'*
Homage to Roy Jenkins, Labour statesman, writer and
wine lover who supposedly kept a space in his minister-
ial diary for 'conjugal rights'.

- *noun* lengthy narrative poem about the historic achievements of
great men or women who in their dealings with the gods gave
shape to the moral universe. From Latin *epicus*, from Greek *epos*
'story, poem'

- see also **Disraeli and Achilles, egotistical glory-mania, feline prowlings, satyriasis, wenching**

Epiphenomena

'For several decades it has been fashionable to say that these so-called great men and women are just epiphenomena, meretricious bubbles on the vast tides of social history … [Churchill] is a pretty withering retort to all that malarkey.'
The Churchill Factor, 2014.

Challenging the view that individual leaders have a limited effect on events.

- *noun* secondary effect or by-product; from Greek *epi* 'on top of', *phainómenon* 'an observable fact or event'
- see also **anaphora, chiasmus, megalopsychia, numen, orotund, spillikin, syllogism, transmogrifying, Zeus and Polyhymnia**

Epiphytes

'It is when you hear Matthew Pinsent speaking, and watch the audience reaction, that you feel your littleness. What are we politicians and journalists? Just parasites, epiphytes upon our national culture.'
Friends, Voters, Countrymen, 2001.

On Olympic rowing champion Matthew Pinsent.

- *noun* a plant that grows on another plant; from Greek *epi* 'on top of', *phuton* 'plant'
- see also **tits in a wringer**

Equo ne credite, Teucri

'In some places it is still the custom to mark any great crisis by consulting Virgil. Close your eyes and jab. For instance, if your finger lights on equo ne credite, Teucri, *you don't bet on the 4.15 at Doncaster.'*

The Spectator, 7 April 2001.

- Borisism
- Latin, 'do not trust the horse, Trojans'. Virgil continues, 'I fear Greeks bearing gifts'. The story of the wooden horse in Virgil's *Aeneid*
- see also **Aegyptia coniunx, nec tali auxilio, nec defensoribus istis, nostos, scandal in the wind, soi-disant poet**

Eudaimonia

'Was it eudaimonia, euphoria, eupepsia or some other Greek word beginning with eu?'

Speech to Conservative Party conference, 9 October 2012.

Hailing the success of the London Olympics as London Mayor.

- *noun* happiness, excitement, well being; from Greek *eu* 'well', *daimon* 'guardian spirit'; euphoria, 'good bearing'; eupepsia, good digestion
- see also **gobsmacked, Pindaric, switcheroo, vaginal endearment, wet otters, wiff-waff, zoink**

Europa

'I do not know whether any hon. Members are foolish enough to oppose eventual Turkish membership of the EU. If so, I ask them where they think Europa was when she was

raped by the bull? … She was on the Turkish coast, one of the many reasons Turkey ultimately has a European vocation.'

House of Commons, 21 May 2003.

Debating EU expansion.

- From Greek mythology; Phoenician princess abducted from the Augean coast by Zeus (taking the form of a white bull) and taken to Crete
- see also **Aryan bull pig**, **Prometheus**, **Zeus and Polyhymnia**

Eurydice

'Cameron was going to probe the belly of the beast and bring back British sovereignty, like Hercules bringing back Eurydice from the underworld.'

Daily Telegraph (unpublished), 19 February 2016.

From his infamous unpublished article arguing to remain in the UK, on how David Cameron had failed to win concessions from the EU.

- It was actually Orpheus, not Hercules, who tried to bring his dead wife Eurydice back from the underworld in Greek mythology
- see also **Bremain**, **Cincinnatus**, **demotic**, **girly swot**, **toad beneath the harrow**

Excogitates

'She soon comes back to life, and with geisha-like deference, excogitates your next move.'

Life in the Fast Lane, 2007.

On a female-voiced sat nav.

- *verb* to think out, to devise; from Latin *ex-* 'out', *cogitare* 'think'

- see also **expenses chicks, gynaecomorphised**

Execration

'Thousands of young people were hurling execration at my name. It took Margaret Thatcher ten years before she had mobs of urban youth denouncing her.'
Wall Street Journal, 3 January 2009.

On the hostile reaction to his plan to outlaw drinking on public transport as Mayor of London.

- *noun* curse; from Latin *ex-* 'out', *sacrare* 'to devote to holiness or to destruction'
- see also **hogwhimpering, sclerotic**

Expenses chicks

'The chicks in the GQ *expenses department – and if you can't call them chicks, then what the hell, I ask you, is the point of writing for GQ? – decided to put their perfectly formed feet down.'*
Life in the Fast Lane, 2007.

On driving a Bentley.

- see also **Araminta, gynaecomorphised, Italian stallion, tinplate testosterone, two-seater chickwagon**

Exsanguinating

'He was sitting in the back, by the exsanguinating form of…'
Seventy-Two Virgins, 2004.

- *verb* to exsanguinate; a person or animal being drained of blood. From Latin *exsanguinatus* 'drained of blood'

F

Faggot

'He yodelled at Matt … "Don't you touch me, you faggot!"'
Seventy-Two Virgins, 2004.

- *noun* derogatory term for a homosexual male. Origin unknown; possibly from 'fag', term for younger boys who performed duties (sometimes sexual) for older boys in English public schools, or shortening of 'faggot-gatherer', those who gathered and sold firewood
- see also **consecrated**, **Taliban chappies**, **tank-topped bumboys**, **up the Arcelor**

Fantastic goer

'Theodora was the world's first international porn star … also the most fantastic goer … Her pièce de resistance was to lie down on stage in a g-string, while specially trained geese would peck morsels from between her legs.'
The Dream of Rome, 2006.

- Theodora (c. 500 AD–548 AD) was the wife of Byzantine Emperor Justinian (482 AD–565 AD); before her marriage, she was an actress and prostitute

- see also **fornicating, Palestinian doxy, Paris Hilton, poule de luxe, sexpot adventuress, sexually liberated, sharmoota, wenching**

Fasti

'Important businessmen and powerful lawyers in ancient Rome sometimes wanted to transact business on the fasti, and it was important to decide whether business could, or could not, take place on the fasti. There was a sort of "Keep Fasti Special" campaign in those days.'

House of Commons, 16 May 2003.

Debating Sunday trading laws.

- Borisism
- *noun* calendars in Ancient Rome which recorded dates of religious or official significance; from Latin *fas* 'legitimate in the eyes of the gods'
- see also **hebdomadal, Solon**

Feckless

'The modern British male is useless. If he is blue collar, he is likely to be drunk, criminal, aimless, feckless and hopeless, and perhaps claiming to suffer from low self-esteem brought on by unemployment.'

The Spectator, August 1995.

On the social breakdown of working-class communities.

- *adjective* lacking strength of character; from Scots and northern English dialect *feck* 'effect' and 'less'; sixteenth century

- see also **banana-booted demigod, chavs, hogwhimpering, Jackson Pollocked, Maenads, piss-head, sjambok, surefire destitution**

Feline prowlings

'Wilkes still conducted feline prowlings between the houses of his various mistresses and offspring, but he also managed to be an efficient and well-paid chamberlain of the City while producing editions of Catallus and Theophrastus.'
The Spirit of London, 2012.

On how eighteenth-century journalist, radical and MP John Wilkes found time for mistresses and illegitimate children in addition to his prolific career as a scholar and politician.

- Borisism
- Theophrastus, Greek philosopher (371 BC–287 BC)
- see also **divine lewdness, epic poem, larks' tongue patties, militia amoris, satyriasis, wenching**

Filching

'If the fuel strikers had not struck, people would never have grasped so clearly how much money Gordon [Brown] is filching.'
Daily Telegraph, 2 November 2000.

On fuel tax protests.

- *verb* to steal or pilfer; from Middle English; origin unknown
- see also **asphodel and mallow, gelatinous, Gordonomics, protoplasmic invertebrate jellies, trud**

Fink

'If he had been asked to do a word association test, and you had said the word "British", he would have said "rat" or "fink" or "shithead".'

Seventy-Two Virgins, 2004.

A US soldier asked to describe the average Briton.

* *verb* American slang for informer, or someone held in contempt. From German *fink* 'finch', bird, used pejoratively to describe an outsider; possibly linked to finches being uncaged birds

Flaccidity

'Her eight months in England had been an unremitting tale of tepidity, frustration, and … flaccidity. She had been taken on "dates" only to find that the man's idea of a romantic climax was to escort her to a bar and meet a couple of his "mates" from "school" … Charterhouse or Bradfield or some other fee-paying haven of hunnish practices.'

Seventy-Two Virgins, 2004.

A female character blaming men from certain public schools (notably, not Johnson's alma mater Eton!) for her sexual frustration.

* *noun* flaccidity, limp; lacking firmness; from Latin *flaccidus* 'flabby'. Hunnish practices, slang, depraved sexual behaviour by men. The soldiers of Attila the Hun, who defeated the Romans, were known for rape and pillage
* see also **donger, non-turgor factor, one-eyed trouser snake, phallocratic phallus**

Flag-waving piccaninnies

'It is said that the Queen has come to love the Common-wealth, partly because it supplies her with regular cheering crowds of flag-waving piccaninnies.'

Daily Telegraph, 10 January 2002.

- *noun* offensive term for a small black child. From West Indies patois, Portuguese *pequenino* 'very small'
- see also **dusky, half-caste, Hottentot, part-Kenyan ancestral dislike, puffing coolies**

Flinty

'All the young people I know are just as avaricious as we flinty Thatcherite yuppies of the 1980s.'

The Spectator, 1999.

- *adjective* hard and unyielding person; from English sixteenth century, as hard as a piece of flint
- see also **acnoid, Ambrosia, execration, sclerotic**

Flobbery

'A slobbering, sexist xenophobe ... Veins bulging and a sheen of sweat appearing on his brow; and yet such natural charisma that women sought the right to sit next to him, and men of power would ... hope some pearl would fall from his flobbery lips ... A genius ... Would he have been allowed to write a column today, with all his exuberant rudeness? I doubt it.'

Daily Telegraph, 14 September 2009.

On Dr Samuel Johnson.

- *adjective* eighteenth-century Scottish slang, dirty, slovenly
- see also **epic poem, phallocratic phallus, pudding basin, satyriasis**

Fornicating

'Vanessa with the sweet white smile and the fat red kissy lips, whom he had trusted with his heart, and who had turned out to be a fornicating traitor.'
Seventy-Two Virgins, 2004.

- *verb* to fornicate; sex between people who are not married to each other; from Latin *fornix* 'vaulted chamber', later 'brothel'
- see also **fantastic goer, wenching**

Fuck business

Overheard at an event for EU diplomats in London, June 2018.
Johnson was said to have used the exclamation as Foreign Secretary at a diplomatic gathering to brush off claims by some business leaders about the economic impact of a no-deal Brexit.

- Borisism
- see also **autarkic, boosterism, Bre-entry, gloomadon-poppers, stuffed, whey**

Führerprinzip

'The purpose of this Führerprinzip is, as Blair has boasted himself, to evoke comparisons with the last apparently visionary leader of this country, Mrs Thatcher. And that is where the comparison comes unstuck.'
Daily Telegraph, 27 August 1997.

On Tony Blair as the new Margaret Thatcher.

- *noun* the basis of Adolf Hitler's rule; German meaning 'leader principle'; dictator 'born to rule'
- see also **acnoid, Archaiser, Caligula gleam, drag artistry, gestapo-ed, Neronian, pater patriae, phenotype**

Fully extended bonk

'You can twizzle your seat up, down, forwards and back as though working your way through a sex manual with an uncomplaining and untiring partner ... the dentist's chair, buttock-clencher for fast driving, and the fully extended bonk position.'

Life in the Fast Lane, 2007.

Reviewing a Mercedes.

- Borisism
- see also **Dorking Rugby Club's second XV, expenses chicks, gynaecomorphised, poule de luxe, two-seater chickwagon**

Fungible

'What I hated about Brussels was not just our national impotence, but the lying, our lying. Thatcher's, Major's and Blair's ministers would come out to Brussels, do a little drum roll about how they were going to fight ... then surrender. It was all fungible. All up for grabs.'

Friends, Voters, Countrymen, 2001.

On observing British negotiations in the EU.

- *adjective* goods replaceable by another identical item; mutually interchangeable. From Latin *fungi vice* 'serve in place of'

- see also **Bwussels, give a monkey's, power squiggles, Procruste-an squeezing, vinegarish**

Funkapolitan

'A great jiving funkapolitan melting-pot.'

Speech at Conservative Party conference, 2 October 2016.

- Borisism
- *adjective* a blend of 'funky' and 'cosmopolitan' to describe the young, hip, multicultural modern arts scene in London and, more broadly, the city as a whole. 'Funky', music with a strong dance rhythm, modern and stylish clothing; 'jive', popular dance
- see also **funky Gibbon, most jiving party**

Funky Gibbon

'Sometimes Churchill could be Gibbonian; sometimes he was more of a funky Gibbon.'

The Churchill Factor, 2014.

Describing Churchill's chequered political career.

- Borisism
- 'Funky Gibbon', a 1970s song by British comedy group The Good-ies, involved a dance move of flailing one's arms like a monkey in an erratic way. 'Gibbonian' refers to Edward Gibbon, the eighteenth-century English historian, politician and writer, author of *The History of the Decline and Fall of the Roman Empire*
- see also **dash of Dawson, syllogism, Zeus and Polyhymnia, zingers**

G

Gelatinous

'You great big quivering gelatinous invertebrate jelly of indecision, you marched your troops to the top of the hill in ... 2007. Show us you've got enough guts to have an election. Gordon: Man or Mouse?!'

Wall Street Journal, 3 January 2009.

On Gordon Brown's decision not to call a snap election in 2007.

- *adjective* jelly-like; probably from French *gelatineux*
- see also **asphodel and mallow, filching, Gordonomics, protozoan, trud**

Gestapoed

'An ever-growing proportion of British women have been ... socially gestapoed into the workplace, on the dubious assumption that the harder a woman works the happier she will be.'

Lend Me Your Ears, 2003.

- Borisism

- *verb* 'to gestapo'; forced to work against their will'; from German *Geheime Staatspolizei* (Secret State Police), abbreviated to Gestapo, the official secret police agency of Nazi Germany and German-occupied Europe
- see also **Führerprinzip, Goebbels-esque fallaciousness, trud**

Get Agrippa

'If Emperor Augustus had any kind of logistical or military problem, his first reaction, I imagine, was to shout, "Get Agrippa".'

- Borisism
- Marcus Vipsanius Agrippa (64 BC–12 BC) was a Roman consul, statesman and general. He was Emperor Augustus's great friend and counsel, as well as the architect of some of his greatest military victories
- see also **midfield playmaker, Octavian the cornflake, pater patriae**

Gibbering rictus

'You feel as if your buttocks have been suddenly clamped by the leather seat ... I had the impression that my face was being pushed back into a gibbering rictus as the G-forces kicked in ... like a man who had slipped the bonds of civilization and rediscovered his bestial soul.'

Life in the Fast Lane, 2007.

On driving fast.

- *noun* open mouthed with fear; from Latin *rictus* 'open mouthed'
- see also **auto-flagellation, buttock exposure, consecrated,**

gynaecomorphised, Italian stallion, rictus of amazement, two-seater chickwagon, unclove

Gibbonian

'There was nothing to tell you who or what had built this place, and as I sat there in Gibbonian contemplation, I reflected on the relative durability of great literature and great buildings.'

The Dream of Rome, 2006.

- Borisism
- *adjective* contemplating in the manner of English historian Edward Gibbon (1737–94), author of *The History of the Decline and Fall of the Roman Empire*
- see also **funky Gibbon**

Gift of death

'Another one, high, fast – it was a miracle. I gave that bird the gift of death, as Hemingway puts it. A feeling of elation flooded through. Bill was approaching with the pheasant and daubing blood on my forehead.'

Daily Telegraph, 6 February 1999.

The thrill of shooting a pheasant.

- Ernest Hemingway said suspending the imagination and living in the moment was a soldier's 'greatest gift' because it conquered cowardice
- see also **akratic, Brueghelian, cauls, gralloched, semolina blob, sexual yipping, Tiglath-Pileser, tweed-wearing atavism**

Gigabucks

'Has it made our lives better by pouring gigabucks into a not-for-profit morass called Network Rail, a leaderless, directionless, state-owned invertebrate, run with all the panache and market sensitivity of a gumboot factory in communist Bulgaria?'

Daily Telegraph, 3 July 2003.

On money spent on the railways by the Blair government.

- *noun* a lot of money; from Greek *giga* 'giant'
- see also **bugger, crapshoot, protoplasmic invertebrate jellies**

Ginormous convocation

'They are chomping remorselessly through the London clay and they are going to meet somewhere for this ginormous convocation of worms.'

Speech at Conservative Party conference, 30 September 2013.

Describing underground diggers excavating London's Crossrail.

- Borisism
- *noun* large formal assembly of people; ginormous, from English 'giant'; convocation, from Latin *convocato* 'convene, convoke'

Girly swot

'The whole September session is a rigmarole introduced by girly swot Cameron to show the public that MPs were earning their crust.'

Hand-written description of David Cameron in the margin of a Cabinet document, 16 August 2019.

On the row over Johnson's five-week suspension of Parliament to try to force Brexit through.

- *noun* contemptuous term for someone who works hard but is weak
- see also **big girl's blouse, Bremain, Cincinnatus, demotic, Eurydice, toad beneath the harrow**

Give 3Ps a chance

'What we call the 3Ps of peacekeeping ... Planning. Pledges. Performance ... As John Lennon said, let's give the 3Ps a chance.'

Speaking at a UN meeting in London, 8 September 2016.

- Borisism
- Adapted from 'Give Peace a Chance', John Lennon's anti-war anthem
- see also **Bee Gees, Kylie's rear, scandal in the wind**

Give a monkey's

'My boast, and I make it in the confidence that no one gives a monkey's, is that I probably did contribute to the Danish rejection of Maastricht.'

Boris: The Adventures of Boris Johnson, 2016.

Denmark's rejection of the Maastricht Treaty in a 1992 referendum was a blow to EU integration plans. As the *Daily Telegraph*'s Brussels correspondent, Johnson filed a story claiming the treaty was part of a federal masterplan by Jacques Delors, European Commission President. It was said to have affected the Danish vote.

- *idiom* to not give a monkey's, totally unconcerned about

something; slang, less coarse version of 'don't give a monkey's toss'
– the ejaculation of a monkey has no value

- see also **dithyramb, e pluribus unum, fungible, glow-worm transience, homo foederalis, Procrustean squeezing, vinegarish**

Glah-stonbury

'When this weekend the BBC broadcast Glastonbury around the world … It is "Glah-stonbury"; it is in the south-west.'

House of Commons, 26 June 2017.

Stating that the correct pronunciation of the music festival in Somerset, south-west England (not far from the Johnsons' family farm) is 'glass' – not 'glas' as in 'mass'.

- Borisism

Gloomadon-poppers

'I have to tell any lingering gloomadon-poppers that never once have I felt that this country would be in any way disadvantaged by extricating ourselves from the EU treaties.'

Speech at Conservative Party conference, 2 October 2016.

- Borisism
- *noun* his spokesman said it referred to those 'who habitually put out negative news'; wordplay on 'gloom' and the sedative drug Mogadon; 'poppers' is slang for drug users
- see also **boosterism, Bre-entry, Bremain, fuck business, gloomsters, murrain, penumbra**

Gloomsters

'The doubters, the doomsters, the gloomsters...'

First speech as Prime Minister, 24 July 2019.

Describing the people he vowed to prove wrong the day he entered Downing Street.

- Borisism
- *noun* a gloomy, negative person
- see also **boosterism, gloomadon-poppers**

Glow-worm transience

'I asked a 25-year-old *Spectator* colleague whether she knew who Jacques Delors was. "I know the name," she said, cautiously. There, my friends, you have the glow-worm transience of journalism.'

Daily Telegraph, 15 September 2003.

Reflecting on the lack of impact had by all journalists – including himself (he spent years attacking European Commission President Jacques Delors).

- Borisism
- *noun* glow-worms glow brightly during their short lives
- see also **boondoggle, give a monkey's, homo foederalis, suppressio veri and suggestio falsi, swankpot journalists, tits in a wringer**

Gobsmacked

'There we were, little old us, the country that made a Horlicks of the Millennium Dome. Putting on a flawless performance of the most logistically difficult thing you can

ask a country to do in peacetime. Some of us were frankly flabbergasted, gobsmacked.'

Speech at Conservative Party conference, 9 October 2012.

On the success of the 2012 London Olympics.

- *adjective* shocked, astonished, astounded; from English 'gob', slang for mouth, and 'smack', act of clapping one's hand to one's mouth in shock
- see also **bumbling skill**, **cyclotron**, **eudaimonia**, **Pindaric**, **switcheroo**, **zoink**

Goebbels-esque fallaciousness

'In a passage of fascist, Goebbels-esque fallaciousness, he strung together conservatism with the killers of Martin Luther King and Stephen Lawrence. One might as well say that "the Labour party and the forces of socialism" were connected with Stalin's purges.'

The Spectator, 2 October 1999.

Comparing an attack on the Conservatives by Tony Blair to Hitler's propaganda chief Joseph Goebbels.

- *noun* fallaciousness; from Latin *falsus* 'false'
- see also **Archaiser**, **Caligula gleam**, **Führerprinzip**, **gestapoed**, **guff**, **turnip ghost**, **whiffled**

Gordonomics

'The vast Ponzi scheme called Gordonomics, an orgy of consumption, racking up huge debts, on the tacit assumption that they would be met by new entrants to the scheme … our children, and taxpayers unborn…'

Daily Telegraph, 22 December 2008.

On the economic policies of Labour Chancellor Gordon Brown.

- Borisism
- Ponzi scheme, money-making fraud named after Italian swindler Charles Ponzi, who gained notoriety in the US in the 1920s
- see also **asphodel and mallow, filching, gelatinous, guff, shit-or-bust, trud**

Go whistle

'Go whistle seems to me to be an entirely appropriate expression.'

House of Commons, 11 July 2017.

Agreeing with a Tory MP who said that the UK should tell the EU to 'go whistle' over the Brexit 'divorce bill'.

- *idiom* rude way of saying you will not give a person what they have asked for; seafarers' superstition that they could make the wind blow by whistling for it
- see also **autarkic, Bre-entry, polish a turd, simulacrum**

Gralloched

'We were walking along the bank of a river when some hounds brought the stag to bay. In less than a minute the beast had been shot and gralloched on the grass. Zip went the knife, and it all came spilling out, as carefully packed as a silken parachute.'

Life in the Fast Lane, 2007.

On seeing a stag killed and prepared.

- *verb* disembowelled; from Scottish Gaelic *grealach* 'entrails'

- see also **Brueghelian, cauls, gift of death, sexual yipping, Tiglath-Pileser, tweed-wearing atavism**

Greased piglet

'It is just flipping unbelievable. A mixture of Harry Houdini and a greased piglet … barely human in his elusiveness. Nailing Blair is like trying to pin jelly to a wall.'

Daily Telegraph, 29 January 2004.

Describing the report into the death of MoD weapons expert Dr David Kelly, who committed suicide after a row over whether Blair lied about Saddam Hussein's weapons in the run-up to the Iraq War.

- *noun* slippery character; someone evasive
- see also **Archaiser, casus belli, Goebbels-esque fallaciousness, guff, pretzel-words, superannuated taramasalata, witchetty grub**

Guff

'Tony Blair delivered a calculating and confident speech expressed in the hot gospelling-language of the star of a religious rock musical. As a piece of inspirational guff, the speech rated an alpha.'

September 1995.

On Blair's speech to the Labour conference.

- *noun* foolish talk or ideas; from English, early nineteenth century, 'puff, whiff of a bad smell'
- see also **Goebbels-esque fallaciousness, greased piglet, turnip ghost, vanilla nothingness, whiffled**

Guppygate

'I ... don't think I have any skeletons to speak of in my cup-board ... I waited for him to hit me with it and it was the usual thing. Guppygate. You don't know about Guppygate, and you don't care? Good. Let's leave it at that. It is a tale told by an idiot, signifying nothing.'

Friends, Voters, Countrymen, 2001.

On being quizzed over a secretly recorded plot in 1990 to supply a fellow Old Etonian, convicted fraudster Darius Guppy, with the contact details of a journalist so that he could have him beaten up.

- see also **Homeric code, inverted pyramid of piffle**

Gynaecomorphised

'The reader may wish I hadn't ... gynaecomorphised these machines so often, but all I can say is that is how they felt to me.'

Life in the Fast Lane, 2007.

Apologising for his highly sexualised car reviews for *GQ* magazine.

- From Greek *gyne* 'woman'; Greek *morphe* 'form'
- see also **Dorking Rugby Club's second XV, endocrine orchestra, expenses chicks, Italian stallion, phallocratic phallus, poule de luxe, Testadicazzo, two-seater chickwagon**

H

Hair shirt-ism

'That ... is how we will tackle the climate change issue – not with the hair shirt-ism of the Greens but with wonderful new technology made in this country.'

House of Commons, 25 July 2019.

Praising the growth of the UK electric car industry.

- Borisism
- *noun* austerity, self-sacrifice; hairshirt, worn by penitents and ascetics
- see also **Brahmaputra, chitterlings and chine, hempen, Toutatis, vertiginously**

Half-caste

'The interesting thing about his half-caste looks, he decided, was that he didn't look Negroid. He looked kind of Arab: dark skin, curly hair, a forceful but straight nose.'

Seventy-Two Virgins, 2004.

- Offensive racial term
- see also **dusky, Hottentot, Nilotic, puffing coolies, watermelon smiles**

Half-groat

'I spent this morning looking at some of the extraordinary things that are for sale on eBay. A half-groat from the time of Henry VIII was going for only £5.50.'

House of Commons, 26 May 2004.

Debating the illicit trade in antiquities.

- *noun* coin worth two pence used in England in the fifteenth century; from Middle Dutch *groot* 'great, thick', hence thick penny
- see also **maw**

Hebdomadal

'Since the dawn of human civilisation, some days, usually on some hebdomadal rhythm of the kind that we have in our Christian culture, have been reserved for holiday and have been kept special.'

House of Commons, 16 May 2003.

Debating Sunday trading laws.

- *adjective* seven-day week; from Greek *hepta* 'seven'; from Latin *hebdomas/hebdomada* 'seven days'
- see also **Diocletian, fasti, Solon**

Hecatomb

'I gave them a polished account of the crisis so far ... studding my remarks with words like hecatomb and holocaust ... where else do you get to use these words ... in a modern context?'

Friends, Voters, Countrymen, 2001.

On BSE, 'mad cow disease'.

- From Greek *hekatombe*, combination of *hekaton* 'hundred' and

bous 'ox', sacrifice of 100 cattle to the gods; holocaust, the burning of all parts of a sacrificial animal
- see also **Hottentot**

Heisenberg
'A manifestation of Heisenberg's uncertainty principle. It would be disastrous.'
Speech at Conservative Party conference, 3 October 2017.
Mocking Jeremy Corbyn's Brexit policy.
- *noun* in quantum mechanics, according to German scientist Werner Heisenberg's uncertainty principle, the position and velocity of an object cannot both be measured at the same time
- see also **Caracas, hempen, ignoratio elenchi, mutton-headed mugwump**

Hempen
'Let Corbyn and co knit their own hempen vests and make their own toothpaste.'
Daily Telegraph, 9 June 2019.
Responding to Jeremy Corbyn's call to curb business to tackle climate change.
- *adjective* made from hemp fibre
- see also **Brahmaputra, Caracas, chitterlings and chine, Heisenberg, Toutatis, vertiginously**

Hippomonstrosesquippedaliophobia
'Meaningless "hippomonstrosesquippedaliophobia" slogan'
Wording on Boris's jogging T-shirt, 2015.

- *noun* ironically named fear of long words; made up of sesquipe-dalian, from Latin *sesquipedalis* 'a foot and a half long'; *monstrum* 'monster', hippo (intended to exaggerate the length of the word itself), Greek *phobia* 'fear'
- see also **anti-aphrodisiacal, hecatomb, Hottentot**

Hogwhimpering

'*Deep down, because of some peculiarity in our psyche, we think it rather admirable to get bladdered, leathered, rat-arsed and otherwise hogwhimpering drunk.*'
Daily Telegraph, 11 August 2005.
On the British attitude to alcohol.

- *adjective* extreme drunkenness; from American English, 'enough alcohol to make a hog whimper'
- see also **Châteauneuf-du-Pape cabal, clinkie, crapulous, feck-less, Jackson Pollocked, Maenads, piss-heads**

Homeric code

'*He lives by a Homeric code of honour, loyalty and revenge.*'
Daily Telegraph, 1993.
Defending Darius Guppy after he was sentenced to five years in prison.

- *noun* the belief that honour is gained through life-threatening ac-tivities. In Homer's *Iliad* the goal of Homeric heroes is to achieve honour; they must kill or be killed
- see also **Augean, Disraeli and Achilles, Guppygate, nostos**

Homo foederalis

'We are locked into a federation. By deciding ever more in common, the twelve countries have created a supranational federal authority in Brussels. And the exact status of Delors, homo foederalis, has become ever more mysterious.'

The Spectator, 7 December 1991.

One of Boris's favourite targets, European Commission President Jacques Delors and the Maastricht Treaty.

- Borisism
- *noun* a new species; Latin *homo* 'man', Latin *foederalis* 'federal' (with the added twist, intentional or not, of containing 'foe' within it)
- see also **e pluribus unum, fungible, give a monkey's, glow-worm transience, power squiggles, Procrustean squeezing**

Homo sovieticus

'You may still be a welfare state Homo sovieticus, stuck in exactly the same Legoland universe as everyone else. But it is up to you ... to decide which of more than fifty attractions you will grace with your presence, if not your custom.'

Daily Telegraph, 29 July 2004.

Using Legoland to justify reforming the welfare state.

- *noun* dog Latin for 'Soviet man', a sarcastic reference to socialist conformism
- see also **Caracas, dolts and serfs, Lego, painful plastic cuboids, Stakhanovite, trud**

Hongi

'Thank you for teaching me the hongi … though it might be misinterpreted in a pub in Glasgow, if you were to try it.'
Speaking on a visit to New Zealand, 24 July 2017.

- *noun* traditional Maori greeting in which people press their noses together; light-heartedly comparing it to a 'Glasgow kiss', slang for headbutt in Scotland

Horlicks

'The government made a Horlicks of an announcement about new evidence which might link BSE with a fantastically rare human brain disease. This Horlicks was turned into a full-dress disaster by an irrational EU decision to ban British beef.'
1996.

- *idiom* a mess; to 'make a Horlicks' of something is a substitute, mainly in Britain, for the more vulgar 'making a bollocks' of it. Horlicks is a hot malted beverage, similar to Ovaltine
- see also **chitterlings and chine, toxoplasmosis**

Hottentot

'The chap always says "I am now going to call upon so and so to say a few words", and then for an anarchic moment you think, Which words shall I say – Hottentot? Axolotl? Carminative? – and how few can I get away with?'
Friends, Voters, Countrymen, 2001.
Boasting about his speech-making.

- *noun* racial term used by the Dutch in the seventeenth century to refer to the Khoikoi, nomadic tribe in South Africa; from German, hotteren-totteren, stutter, a reference to the clicking sounds in the Khoikoi language. Axolotl, *noun* near-extinct amphibian with a large white head found in Mexico; adopted as a nonsense word by *Mad* magazine. Carminative, *adjective/noun* drug which relieves flatulence; from Latin *carminativum*, a herb used to cure wind

- see also **dusky, half-caste, hecatomb, hippomonstrosesquippedal-iophobia, rictus of amazement**

Hubble-bubble pipe

'*A constituent who recently applied to join the police … was turned down on the ground that he had three tattoos on his upper arms: one of a man waving a flag, one of a dog, and one of a mouse sitting on a toadstool smoking a hubble-bubble pipe.*'
House of Commons, 16 June 2003.

Debating knife crime.

- *noun* water pipe used to smoke shisha tobacco
- see also **narghileh**

Hulk

'*The madder Hulk gets, the stronger Hulk gets.*'
Mail on Sunday, 14 September 2019.

Pledging to break free from EU 'manacles'.

- Borisism
- Fictional superhero from the 1960s Marvel comic and later in two Hollywood movies. Following accidental exposure to gamma rays, mild-mannered Bruce Banner is physically transformed into the raging Hulk when stressed or angry

93

- see also **Bremain**, **Brexchosis**

Human panda

'We could send the human panda to Beijing in the … spirit of discreet sabotage.'

Daily Telegraph, 3 October 2011.

Suggesting Labour leader Ed Miliband should go to China to wreck their economy with his left-wing policies.

- Borisism
- Miliband was caricatured by some cartoonists as a panda
- see also **Sinophobia**

Humbug

'I have never heard such humbug in all my life.'

House of Commons, 25 September 2019.

Retort to Labour MP Paula Sherriff's claim that his 'inflammatory language' on Brexit risked a repeat of the murder of Labour MP Jo Cox in 2016 by a far-right extremist.

- *noun* false talk or behaviour, nonsense; possibly Old Norse, *hum* 'night' or 'shadow', Biblical *bugges* 'apparition'
- see also **cobblers, inverted pyramid of piffle**

Huncho-swingometer

'It is my personal huncho-swingometer, and it has worked well in the past.'

Friends, Voters, Countrymen, 2001.

- Borisism

- *noun* a feeling or guess based on intuition rather than fact; combination of hunch and swingometer, a graphics device used on TV to measure political swings, particularly around election time
- see also **Tottometer**

Hur

'Think of the hur, the black-eyed virgins of Paradise, Dean. Would you like seventy-two black-eyed virgins, whose chastity has been violated neither by man nor djinn?'
Seventy-Two Virgins, 2004.

- *noun* 'maidens' in Islamic notion of Paradise. Djinn, Arabic, broadly interpreted as spirit or demon
- see also **Kulturkampf, pathetic Islamofascists, piss against the wall, raisins, xenophobe**

Hyperpuissance

'Sometimes we become so paranoid about America, which we call the hyperpuissance, that we become exuberant in our language.'
Seventy-Two Virgins, 2004.

On exaggerated fears of US strength.

- *noun* one step up from super power; coined in 1991 by French Foreign Minister Hubert Védrine. From Greek *hyper* 'over, beyond', French *puissance* 'power'
- see also **crack-brained neocons, Sinophobia, stupefying ignorance**

Hypothalamus

'Somewhere in my endocrine system something gave a

little squirt – adrenal gland, pituitary, hypothalamus, and pow, I could feel myself being transformed from this shy, spotty, swotty nerd.'

The Spirit of London, 2012.

On hearing the 1981 Rolling Stones song 'Start Me Up' for the first time as a teenager.

- *noun* part of the brain that stimulates sex drive via endocrine system and pituitary gland; from Greek, *hypo* 'under', *thalamus* 'chamber'; the part of brain where nerves emerge

- see also **bag of ferrets, Bee Gees, endocrine orchestra, Inca mummy, scandal in the wind, spaffed, two-seater chickwagon**

Hyrcanian tiger

'You are like some ravening Hyrcanian tiger deprived of its mortal prey – a Johnson blooper.'

Mail on Sunday, 3 May 2008.

Claiming journalists were frustrated he had won the London mayoral election campaign without giving them any headline-grabbing gaffes.

- The 'ravenous' beasts – believed to be now-extinct Caspian tigers – that roamed the ancient kingdom of Hyrcania, now Iran and part of Turkmenistan. The Hyrcanian tiger features in classical literature. Blooper, 1920s US term for annoying feedback from a badly tuned radio

- see also **charismatic megafauna, mayoral culpa, nel mezzo del cammin di nostra vita, swankpot journalists, tiggerish, Tsavo**

I

'Ich bin ein Frankfurter.'

The Guardian, 24 June 2006.

Used in his first interview as Conservative higher education spokesman to compare himself to 1960s Austrian-American academic freedom campaigner Justice Felix Frankfurter.

- Borisism
- Borrowed from John F. Kennedy's 'ich bin ein Berliner' Cold War speech in West Berlin; Felix Frankfurter was awarded the US Medal of Freedom by JFK
- see also **Spheroids**

Icing sugar

'I think I was once given cocaine but I sneezed so it didn't go up my nose. In fact, I may have been doing icing sugar.'
Have I Got News For You, BBC One, 2005.

- see also **chavs, Inca mummy, most jiving party, nephos, psychotropical effect**

Ignoratio elenchi

'The right hon. Gentleman is showing complete ignoratio elenchi – a complete failure to study what we actually passed last night in that historic agreement.'

House of Commons, 23 October 2019.

Accusing Jeremy Corbyn of missing the point after the government won a Brexit vote.

- *idiom* logical fallacy which consists of apparently refuting an opponent while actually disproving something not asserted; from Latin *ignoratio* 'ignorance'; elenchi, Latin via Greek *elenchos* 'argument of disproof or refutation'
- see also **Caracas, Heisenberg, hempen, mutton-headed mugwump**

Ils sont passes, ces beaux jours

'It has been made clear to Marina she is not expected to turn up for orgies of chutney making … or some ladies' luncheon club where in former times the audience might have been treated to a paper called … "Nothing Wrong With A Loving Smack". Ils sont passes, ces beaux jours."

Friends, Voters, Countrymen, 2001.

On advice from local Conservative officials to wife Marina when he became Henley MP.

- French, 'the glory days are over'
- see also **donnez-moi un break, matricide, Papua New Guinea chief killing, parable of the toast, sac de vomissement, zonk**

Imbecilio

'There's one particular Roman oratorical trick I use the

whole time. Couldn't survive without it ... It's absolutely crucial – it's called imbecilio.'

- *adjective* to put on the pretence of being a fool; weak, foolish; from Latin *imbecillus* 'without support', 'feeble'
- see also **bufferdom, buffoon, bumbling skill, inverted pyramid of piffle, Latinate evasion, wise guy**

Imperial good-time girls
'Some see themselves ... attended by imperial good-time girls and dangling grapes towards their mouths.'
The Dream of Rome, 2006.

On men who fantasise about being Romans.

- *noun* young women who enjoy partying or sex; also prostitutes
- see also **divine gift of lewdness, ecclesiastical bunga-bunga, fantastic goer, feline prowlings, Paris Hilton, sharmoota, wenching**

Impis
"'We want ID cards! We had them in the war! If you've got nothing to hide, you've got nothing to fear!" And they started gurgling and drumming their feet like the impis of Chaka, and I hung my head and gave up.'
Daily Telegraph, 25 November 2004.

Arguing against ID cards.

- *noun* feared Zulu warriors in what is now known as South Africa. Shaka (or Chaka) was a Zulu king at the turn of the nineteenth century; Zulu *impi* 'war, combat'
- see also **breaking and entering, strigil**

Inanition

'The Lib Dems are not just empty. They are a void within a vacuum surrounded by a vast inanition.'

Daily Telegraph, 25 September 2003.

- *noun* lack of mental or spiritual vigour and enthusiasm; from Latin *inanire* 'to make empty'. Churchill derided one of his commanders as showing the 'dead hand of inanition', and said Russia was 'a riddle wrapped in a mystery inside an enigma'
- see also **Cleggster, taxidermy, yellow albatross**

Inca mummy

'Keith has spent decades slurping, shooting and snorting such prodigious quantities of chemicals that he looks as though the stuff has taxidermied his tissues, like some Inca mummy. He was the one that made teenage girls moan like Maenads...'

The Spirit of London, 2012.

On why Rolling Stones guitarist Keith Richards is better than Mick Jagger.

- Borisism
- see also **Bee Gees, hypothalamus, icing sugar, Kylie's rear, Maenads, nephos, psychotropical effect, scandal in the wind**

Indelible spoor

'We not only leave our indelible spoor in the ether but we are ourselves becoming a resource. Click by click, tap by tap. Just as the carboniferous period created the indescribable

wealth – leaf by decaying leaf – of hydrocarbons. Data is the crude oil of the modern economy.'

UN General Assembly, New York, 24 September 2019.

On the challenge of new technology.

- *noun* animal track or scent that cannot be erased; indelible, imperishable; spoor, track or scent of an animal. From Afrikaans via Dutch *spor* 'animal track or droppings'

Infinite sagacity

'I think they will exercise their infinite sagacity and wisdom in not heeding the siren voices of those who try to overturn the democratic decision of this country's people last year.'

House of Commons, 21 February 2017.

Urging voters to ignore attacks on Brexit by Tony Blair and Peter Mandelson.

- *noun* sagacity, limitless wisdom; from Latin *sagax* 'wise'
- see also **fungible, gloomadon-poppers, guff, tank-topped bumboys, timorousness, vanilla nothingness, whiffle**

Inverted pyramid of piffle

'I have not had an affair with Petronella. It is complete balderdash. It is an inverted pyramid of piffle. It is all completely untrue and ludicrous conjecture. I am amazed that people can write this drivel.'

Mail on Sunday, 7 November 2004.

Falsely denying an affair with journalist and socialite Petronella Wyatt. He was sacked from the Conservative front bench by party leader Michael Howard for lying about it.

- Borisism
- *idiom* nonsense; he used the same expression in 2001 to dismiss reports of the Tory Party's demise and in 2003 to brush aside lurid allegations against Prince Charles. Piffle, possibly combination of piddle and trifle, or puff, puff of air
- see also **best of all worlds, cobblers, ker-splonked, Latinate evasion, Scarface, torrents of obfuscation, twaddle**

Italian stallion

'The M3 opened up before me, a long quiet Bonneville flat stretch … it was as though the whole county of Hampshire was lying back and opening her well-bred legs to be ravished by the Italian stallion.'

Life in the Fast Lane, 2007.

On driving a Ferrari.

- Stallion, uncastrated horse; nickname for handsome Italian man; moniker of the Italian-American boxer played by Sylvester Stallone in the *Rocky* movie series
- see also **bag of ferrets, braggadocio, fully extended bonk, gynaecomorphised, phallocratic phallus, pin-goaded stallion, stung in the bum, Testadicazzo**

J

Jabberama

'The great caffeine-powered, keyboard-hammering com-munity of online thinkers who contribute with such richness to the cyberspace jabberama.'

Daily Telegraph, 17 January 2011.

Defending the public's right to use Twitter and other social media to attack public figures.

- Borisism
- *noun* the cacophony of raucous criticism by internet users; from fifteenth-century English 'jabber', imitative
- see also **bibble-babble, engine of Onan, pullulate, Twitter-borne transphobes**

Jackson Pollocked

'It was a coldish night, but everywhere there was a pagan semi-nudity. There were queues to buy kebabs, and the pavements were Jackson Pollocked with the results of eating a kebab on top of eight pints of lager.'

Daily Telegraph, 11 August 2005.

On drunkenness in the streets.

- Borisism
- *verb* to Jackson Pollock, to vomit on the pavement; Jackson Pollock (1912–56) was an abstract expressionist artist
- see also **chunderous, feckless, hogwhimpering, Maenads, piss-heads**

Johnny Turk

'It's not even that the Turks have sallow skin, thick eyebrows, or low foreheads … the reason the richest nations on earth have havered for so long about admitting Johnny Turk to their club is all about … "values". What these politicians mean [is] … Islam.'

The Dream of Rome, 2006.

- *noun* slang for someone from Turkey; derogatory catch-all Victorian term for foreigners, 'Johnny Foreigner'; 'Johnny Turk' developed in the Crimean War against the Ottoman Empire
- see also **Aryan bull pig, Johnson-oglus**

Johnson-oglus

'I am the first member of a thousand generations of Johnsons – or Johnson-oglus, or whatever our Turkish family name was – to sit in this House.'

Friends, Voters, Countrymen, 2001.

A light-hearted allusion to his Turkish roots.

- Oglus was the suffix of the surname of two ruling dynasties in Armenia. Johnson's Turkish great-grandfather, Ali Kemal (1867–1922), a journalist and politician, spoke out against the Turkish genocide in Armenia in the early twentieth century. He was assassinated

- see also **Aryan bull pig, Johnny Turk, nargileh, xenophobe**

Jot and tittle

'She and I are united … in support of every jot and tittle of the Florence speech.'

House of Commons, 7 November 2017.

Affirming his support of Theresa May's Brexit 'red lines' in her speech in Florence, Italy, in September 2017.

- *noun(s)* very small amount; from Greek *iota*, smallest letter in Greek alphabet; tittle, a small dot or pen stroke to signify an abbreviated word or missing letters; term first appears in William Tyndale's translation of the New Testament in 1526
- see also **bottled Brexit, lapidary, muff it, polish a turd, Precambrian, simulacrum**

Jut-jawed and jackbooted

'A jut-jawed and jackbooted tyrant like Mussolini.'

The Churchill Factor, 2014.

- *noun* jackboot, tall leather military boot worn by the German and Italian armies in the Second World War; jut-jawed, term commonly used to describe Italian dictator Benito Mussolini, who, like Hitler, often wore jackboots; jackbooted, jack, Arabic and Catalan via French *jaque* 'mail' (armour); earlier winged leather cavalry boots were 'jacked', i.e. reinforced against sword blows with mail
- see also **Führerprinzip, Goebbels-esque fallaciousness, platitudinous Pooters, quislings**

K

Ker-splonked

'Nothing excites compassion, in friend and foe alike, as much as the sight of you ker-splonked on the Tarmac with your propeller buried six feet under ... My friends, as I have discovered myself, there are no disasters, only opportunities. And, indeed, opportunities for fresh disasters.'

Daily Telegraph, 2 December 2004.

After he was fired from the Tory front bench for lying about his affair with Petronella Wyatt.

- Borisism
- *verb* humiliated; imitative, variation of 'kerplunk', the thud of something landing noisily; also a game
- see also **best of all worlds, inverted pyramid of piffle, mayoral culpa, snooks**

Kulturkampf

'[I have been] asked to make judgements, as Mayor, about some of the most bitterly contested battlegrounds of our national Kulturkampf.'

3 June 2008.

Commenting on the controversial 'Fourth Plinth' in Trafalgar Square, London, featuring contemporary sculptures, which later included a giant blue cock (or rooster).

- *noun* culture war; from German *Kultur* 'culture', *Kampf* 'struggle'; the term derives from the 1870s conflict between the government of the Kingdom of Prussia and the Roman Catholic Church over educational and religious appointments

- see also **acculturated, piss against the wall, re-Britannification, verkrampte**

Kylie's rear

'When one of the [Lords] dies they should elect someone to fill his or her place. A solution as beautiful as the two halves, symmetrical but wholly anatomically distinct, of the rear end of Kylie Minogue.'

Daily Telegraph, 30 January 2003.

On House of Lords reform.

- Borisism

- see also **bottom pat, buttock exposure, Schindler, Stilton-eating surrender monkeys, tattooed bottoms**

L

Lachrymose

'This lachrymose defence of the Union comes a little ill from somebody who … campaigned to break up the Union between Great Britain and Northern Ireland by his support of the IRA.'
23 October 2019.

Pouring scorn on Labour leader Jeremy Corbyn's claim that Brexit would undermine the United Kingdom.

- *adjective* tearful; from Latin *lacrima* 'tear'
- see also **Caracas, Heisenberg, hempen, ignoratio elenchi, mutton-headed old mugwump**

Laggard

'Laggard 11-year-olds will be forced to attend a three-week intensive literacy course in the summer. Which seems to be a fresh intrusion of the state into family life.'
Daily Telegraph, 2 October 1996.

On the social authoritarianism of Tony Blair.

- *noun* a person who makes slow progress; from English 'lag', to fall behind

Lapidary

'It would be absurd, as Theresa May said in her Lancaster House and Florence speeches – which now have the lapidary status of the codes of Hammurabi or Moses – if we were obliged to obey laws over which we have no say and no vote.'
Speech, February 2018.

Accusing Theresa May of not sticking to her Brexit 'red lines'.

- *adjective* set in stone; the cutting or polishing of stones; from Latin *lapis* 'stone'. Hammurabi, King of Babylon; Moses, Hebrew prophet who led the Israelites out of Egyptian slavery, and received the Ten Commandments, written on stone tablets, from God
- see also **bottled Brexit**, **jot and tittle**, **muff**, **polish a turd**, **simulacrum**, **Solon**

Larks' tongue patties

'It was like being a Visigoth turning up in Rome and being invited to take supper with a senator from one of the older families. He offers you peacock stuffed with dormice, followed by larks' tongue patties, and asks what you think of his statue of Apollo, have you read Catallus?'
Life in the Fast Lane, 2007.

On feeling overwhelmed by the sophistication of a new Mercedes.

- *noun* lark tongue, peacock tongue and stuffed dormice were Roman delicacies. Apollo was a god in Greek and Roman mythology; Catallus was a Roman poet (84 BC–54 BC) renowned for explicit sexual imagery; the Visigoths were a Germanic people who sacked Rome in 410 AD

Lascivious matrons

'The lascivious matrons of Rome would make much of this general and offer to have his babies.'

The Dream of Rome, 2006.

- *adjective* feeling or exhibiting an overt sexual interest or desire; from late Latin *lasciviosus* 'lustful, lustfulness'; initially used in a scolding sense by some early Church writers
- see also **divine gift of lewdness, epic poem, fornicating, imperial good-time girls, sexpot adventuress, wenching**

Latinate evasion

'The thing about Latinate words is they're evasive. Alan Clark used the device brilliantly in the Scott Inquiry. "I was economical with the truth" isn't just brilliant. It's also less self-condemnatory than "I lied."'

Speaking at a Latin-themed charity evening hosted by former *Daily Telegraph* editor Charles Moore, 2007.

- see also **inverted pyramid of piffle, puffing coolies, sandpapered, Scarface, tinplate testosterone**

Lego

'Crumbling fortifications with Lego-like layers of pink and buff masonry...'

The Dream of Rome, 2006.

Describing clambering over the ruins of the ancient walls built to protect Constantinople (Istanbul).

- 'Lego' is the name given to the colourful interlocking blocks produced by the Danish company of the same name. The inventor gave them this name in 1934 as an amalgamation of the Danish phrase *leg godt* meaning 'play well'. It is assumed he did not realise that 'Lego' also means 'I choose', 'I collect' or 'I read' in Latin
- see also **Europa, Homo sovieticus, hubble-bubble pipe, Johnny Turk, Johnson-oglus, narghileh, painful plastic cuboids**

Lighten up, Muslims
'Why couldn't these Muslims just lighten up a little? Hadn't they heard of free speech?'
The Dream of Rome, 2006.
On the terror attacks by Islamic extremists in 2006 when Pope Benedict XVI was accused of insulting Islam.
- see also **acculturated, burqa, Kulturkampf, xenophobe**

Limbless mendicants
'I don't think it's just the result of some Potemkin style clean-up that there are fewer beggars knocking on your window at the traffic lights, fewer limbless mendicants scooting on tea-trays...'
Daily Telegraph, 9 January 2011.
On the booming Indian economy.
- *noun* limbless beggar; from Latin *mendicus* 'beggar'
- see also **Potemkin objects**

Literae humaniores

'One man's Mickey Mouse is another man's literae humaniores.'

Interview in *The Guardian*, 24 June 2006.

Defending non-academic courses in universities.

- *noun* Classics degree devoted to literature, history, philosophy, languages and the archaeology of ancient Greece and Rome – Johnson's degree at Oxford. From Latin *literae* 'literature'; Latin *humaniores* 'more humane'

Little Britons

'There is a lovely tablet … on Hadrian's Wall in which a group of Belgian soldiers speaks disparagingly of the Britunculi – Little Britons. That's right: Brits being disparaged by Belgies.'

The Dream of Rome, 2006.

- Borisism
- a play on the name of the satirical British TV show *Little Britain*
- see also **acculturated, antepartum, pusillanimously, xenophobe**

Little otter

2019.

Said to be Boris's nickname for girlfriend Carrie Symonds.

- Ms Symonds is an animal rights campaigner
- see also **gralloched, sexual yipping, wet otters**

Lobster

'The EU would be a lobster … because the EU, by the very way it works, encourages its participating members to order

the lobster at the joint meal because they know that the bill is going to be settled by everybody else – normally the Germans.'
Daily Telegraph, 12 May 2004.

On the creature the EU most resembles.

- Borism
- see also **boondoggle, Bre-entry, homo foederalis, raw prawn**

Lolling rakes

'When we close our eyes and think of the eighteenth century, we see coffee houses, 3am revels, women talking back for the first time in history, rakes lolling against the bared bosoms of fan waving beldames…'
The Spirit of London, 2012.

- *noun* dissolute men; from 'rake', short for 'rakehell', 'hellraiser'
- see also **divine gift of lewdness, ecclesiastical bunga-bunga**

Lurve

'Antony has come down to us as the pre-eminent example of the man who lost it all for lurve. We remember him as the man who became the bellows and the fan to cool a gypsy's lust.'
The Dream of Rome, 2006.

On Mark Antony and Cleopatra.

- *noun* slushy way of pronouncing 'love'. References to 'the bellows and fan' and 'a gypsy's lust' are from Shakespeare's play *Antony and Cleopatra*
- see also **Aegyptia coniunx, bosky, Burton–Taylor smooching, ceaseless carnal activity, lascivious matrons, whiffled**

M

Maenads

*'A woman was sitting opposite me in a state of some dishevel-
ment. She was extremely good-looking and had a tattoo of a
butterfly on her bosom, but she was pretty far gone. Not since
Pentheus was ripped limb from limb by the Maenads have we
seen such drink-fuelled aggression from the female sex.'*

Daily Telegraph, 11 August 2005.

Criticising Labour plans to liberalise drinking laws after
he was threatened in a pub in Carlisle.

- *noun* drunken woman; Maenad, 'raving one', from Greek *mainesthai*
  'to rave'; Maenads were the female followers of Dionysus, the ancient
  Greek god of wine. They would get into a state of ecstatic frenzy from
  drinking; the Maenads killed King Pentheus and tore his body to pieces
- see also **feckless**, **hogwhimpering**, **Jackson Pollocked**, **piss-
  heads**, **sjambok**

Marmalised

*'If I had said such a thing to any of my teachers I would
not only have had my mobile officially marmalised.'*

Daily Telegraph, 26 October 2009.

Calling for tougher discipline in schools.

- *verb* beaten up; pulverised; from 1980s English, combination of 'marmalade' and 'pulverise'
- see also **encephalopathic**

Matricide

'There is no need to here rehearse the steps of matricide. Howe pounced, Heseltine did his stuff. After it was all over, my wife Marina claimed she came upon me, stumbling down a street in Brussels, tears in my eyes, and claiming that it was as if someone had shot Nanny.'

Lend Me Your Ears, 2003.

On Mrs Thatcher's downfall.

- *noun* the killing of one's mother; from Latin *mater* 'mother', *-cide* 'a person or object who kills; an act of killing'
- see also **acnoid, Ambrosia, flinty, ils sont passes, ces beaux jours, parable of the toast, sclerotic, Simba**

Maw

'During the digging up ... who knows what things will be found? It would be very sad if that archaeological site were destroyed. It would be even sadder if the things that were discovered ... disappeared into the great magnetic maw of eBay.'

Speaking at Westminster Hall, 26 May 2004.

Debating the illegal trade in antiquities.

- *noun* jaws or throat of a fiercely hungry animal; from German *magen* 'stomach'

- see also **half-groat, Panathenaic frieze**

Mayoral culpa

'Mayoral culpa, mayoral maxima culpa.'

March 2012.

Apology as London Mayor after calling the annual St Patrick's Day Gala Dinner, held at the Dorchester in London, 'Sinn Féin lefty crap'.

- Borisism
- *mea culpa* is Latin for 'my fault'; *mea maxima culpa* is Latin for 'my fault in a big way'
- see also **imbecilio, ker-splonked, pilgrim of penitence**

Mazzard

'If BP shares go down then that is bad news for UK pensioners and a tremendous thwack on the mazzard for UK plc.'

Daily Telegraph, 17 September 2012.

- *noun* mazzard, slang term for head, skull; cherry tree known for hard wood; thwack, late Middle English, imitative

Media ectoplasm

'There was never a proposition for general sanctions against Russia … That was a piece of media ectoplasm.'

House of Commons, 18 April 2017.

Debating Vladimir Putin's foreign policy.

- Borisism
- *idiom* fake eruption of fury; ectoplasm, supernatural viscous

substance supposed to exude from body of a medium during a trance. From Greek *ektos* 'outside', *plasma* 'something formed or moulded'

- see also **Dobby, torrents of obfuscation**

Medieval on their ass

'He didn't accept – as Blair did – that these so-called "causes" deserved to be tackled as vigorously as crime itself. That was a limp-wristed cop-out. The causes of crime were criminals, and he cracked down on them. In the phrase of Quentin Tarantino, he got medieval on their ass.'

Daily Telegraph, 2 September 2004.

On former New York Mayor (later senior Trump aide) Rudy Giuliani's tough anti-crime methods and refusal to let criminals blame social causes.

- *idiom* to use medieval-style torture; from Quentin Tarantino's film *Pulp Fiction*; gang leader Marsellus Wallace threatens to torture a victim 'with a pair of pliers and a blow torch' – 'I'm gonna get medieval on your ass.'

- see also **Britannia's ass, hubble-bubble pipe, Mexican stand-off, pegged, scum, sjambok**

Megalopsychia

'Churchill's megalopsychia, greatness of heart.'

The Churchill Factor, 2014.

On how Churchill's artistic talent was part of his depth and appeal.

- *noun* big-hearted, magnanimous; from Greek philosopher Aristotle's definition of virtue; Greek *megalópsūkhos* 'great-souled man'

- see also **funky Gibbon, Gibbonian, syllogism, transmogrifying, Zeus and Polyhymnia, zingers**

Mega-titted

'As she rose, with water running down her terrifying shape, he would assume she was a divinity, a Venus Anadyomene, a mega-titted six-footer.'
Seventy-Two Virgins, 2004.

- *adjective* woman with large breasts. From Greek *megas* 'great, mighty'; *Anadyomene*, Greek 'rising from the sea', *Venus Anadyomene*, 1520 painting by Titian
- see also **Boobtropolis, buxom as all get out, multiple-bosomed, soutien-gorges, tits in a wringer, Tottometer**

Mexican stand-off

'[The Nuclear Non-Proliferation Treaty] has helped avoid what might otherwise have been a Gadarene Rush to destruction, in which the world was turned into a great arena of Mexican stand-offs, a nuclear version of the final scene of Reservoir Dogs.*'*
Speech at Chatham House think tank, 23 October 2017.

- *noun* confrontation among two or more parties in which no one can achieve victory, and no one can get out without losing. Believed to originate in an 1876 story about an American held up by a bandit in Mexico. Quentin Tarantino's *Reservoir Dogs* ends in a bloody confrontation where everyone is shooting at each other
- see also **medieval on their ass, pegged, Scarface, sword of Damocles**

Midfield playmaker

'If you wanted to create a First XI of history's world-class statesmen, you'd pick Augustus as your midfield playmaker.'
The Dream of Rome, 2006.

- *noun* a football player responsible for dictating and initiating the attacking moves of a team
- see also **banana-booted demigod, get Agrippa, namby-pamby, Octavian the cornflake**

Militia amoris

'Whatever you think of his own militia amoris … he did something far worse than fathering two children with a married woman. He told the nation his dog could do a better job than most Labour Cabinet ministers.'
Daily Telegraph, 16 December 2004.

On the resignation of Home Secretary David Blunkett, who is blind, after allegations concerning an affair with married *Spectator* publisher Kimberley Fortier, including fathering a child by her.

- *noun* warfare of love, a popular metaphor for Roman poets comparing romantic conquest to military conquest; from Latin *miles* 'soldier', *militia* 'military service'; *amoris* 'love'
- see also **bottom pat, feline prowlings, pax vobiscum!, satyriasis**

Millennialist suicide cult

'Spending an hour with the FT is like being trapped in a room with assorted members of a millennialist suicide cult.'
Daily Telegraph, 14 October 2008.

Deriding the *Financial Times* for predicting a 1930s-style recession.

- *noun* millennialism, belief advanced by some religious groups that a Golden Age will occur on Earth prior to the final judgment; some committed mass suicide. From Latin *millennium* '1,000 years'
- see also **epiphytes, glow-worm transience, nel mezzo del cammin di nostra vita, pshaw**

Mimetic genius

'She had the mimetic genius for seeing a man's interests and pretending, expertly, to share them.'
The Dream of Rome, 2006.
On Cleopatra's powers of seduction.

- *adjective* having an aptitude for imitation; from Latin *mimus* 'mime actor', Greek *mimētikos* 'good at imitating'
- see also **Aegyptia coniunx, Burton–Taylor smooching, ceaseless carnal activity, lurve, mother-bonking, Paris Hilton**

Minestrone of observations

'A great minestrone of observations.'
At the launch of his Conservative leadership campaign, 12 June 2019.
Trying to avoid being questioned by BBC political editor Laura Kuenssberg over whether he could be 'trusted'.

- Borisism
- minestrone, a thick vegetable soup
- see also **inverted pyramid of piffle, Latinate evasion, obiter dicta**

Monochrome Manichaean

'A man so serially incompetent that he only narrowly escaped self assassination by pretzel ... Who on earth, I moaned, can conceivably have supported this maniac with his monochrome Manichaean rhetoric ... ? Then I remembered. I backed him.'

Daily Telegraph, 4 November 2004.

On waking up to learn that George W. Bush had won a second term.

- *adjective* simplistic, black-and-white view of the world; from Greek *monokhromatos* 'single colour'; Manichaeism, a major religion of late antiquity founded by the Iranian prophet Mani, which broke everything down into good or evil
- see also **buzzard squint, crack-brained neocons, dada-ist, pretzel words**

Monomaniacal

'They have the highest taxes in the UK. They are not running either health or education well. That is why they are so monomaniacal about independence and smashing the Union.'

House of Commons, 31 October 2019.

On Scotland's ruling Scottish National Party.

- *adjective* insane pursuit of one cause; from Greek *monos* 'single' or 'alone'; Greek *mania* 'madness'

Monosyllabic Austrian cyborg

'It was a low moment ... to have my speaking style criticised by a monosyllabic Austrian cyborg.'

Speaking at Conservative Party conference, 28 September 2008.

On unflattering comments on his cameo role in TV soap *EastEnders* by Austrian-American bodybuilder-turned-actor Arnold Schwarzenegger, whose *Terminator* films feature cyborgs, beings with biological and artificial parts.

- *noun* someone who speaks in a short robotic manner; monosyllabic, from Greek *monos* 'single', *syllabe* 'what is taken together', letters forming a single sound; cyborg, cyber, *cyb* and *org*, organ
- see also **condom stuffed with walnuts, pink-eyed terminators**

Montagues and Capulets

'This is the time when we move on and discard the old labels of Leave and Remain … The very words seem tired – as defunct … as Montagues and Capulets at the end of the play.'
House of Commons, 20 December 2019.

Speaking as MPs finally moved towards approving Brexit.

- Montagues and Capulets, rival families in Shakespeare's tragedy *Romeo and Juliet*
- see also **deracinated, lurve, whiffled**

Moonie spell

'Tesco the destroyer of the old-fashioned high street, Tesco the slayer of small shops, Tesco through whose air-conditioned portals we are all sucked like chaff, as though hypnotised by some Moonie spell.'
Daily Telegraph, 15 July 2008.

On the impact of hypermarkets like Tesco on town centres and local businesses.

- Borisism
- 'Moonies' is a pejorative term for members of the Unification Church religious movement founded by Sun Mying Moon, seen as a cult by many and accused of brainwashing young followers

Mordant paradox

'I long to get on with the job, to see political questions not just as subjects for a few mordant paradoxes or thunderous paragraphs...'

Friends, Voters, Countrymen, 2001.

On starting work as an MP after giving up full-time journalism.

- *noun* using a sharp or biting quality to ridicule seemingly contradictory statements or propositions which may prove to be true. From Latin *mordere* 'to bite'; paradox, Greek *para* 'from', *doxa* 'opinion'
- see also **cursus honorum, Disraeli and Achilles, glow-worm transience, nel mezzo del cammin di nostra vita, pshaw, world king**

Morpheus

'The time between my head hitting the pillow and being folded in the arms of Morpheus is so short ... I don't think I think about anything'

Freakonomics Radio podcast interview, 20 November 2014.

On being asked what he worries about at night.

- Morpheus, Greek god of sleep and dreams
- see also **black abyss, zonk**

Most jiving party

'Cannabis is dangerous, but no more than other perfectly legal drugs. It's time for a rethink, and the Tory Party – the funkiest, most jiving party on Earth – is where it's happening.'

Daily Telegraph, 12 July 2001.

Calling on the Conservatives to consider liberalising drugs laws.

- see also **funkapolitan, funky Gibbon, icing sugar, nephos**

Motability rickshaws

'As you limp homewards, overhauled by Motability rickshaws, you debate which animal the Chevrolet boys had in mind. A stallion perhaps, wild horse of the Camargue. You get home. You look it up. You can't believe it. Camaro is Spanish for a kind of shrimp which just about sums it up.'

Life in the Fast Lane, 2007.

On the slowness of the Chevrolet Camaro.

- Borisism
- Motability cars are specially adapted for disabled drivers; the Motability Scheme charity also provides disabled people with scooters and powered wheelchairs. From Spanish slang *camaro* 'little friend'
- see also **endocrine orchestra, Italian stallion, pin-goaded stallion, Testadicazzo**

Mother-bonking

'George III fat-headedly threw his weight around and

advanced the career of Lord Bute who was rumoured to be romancing his mother. This Hanoverian monarch and his Scottish Old Etonian mother-bonking minister...'

The Spirit of London, 2012.

On reports of an affair between the third Earl of Bute, Prime Minister 1762–63, and the King's mother, Princess Augusta, sparked riots in London.

- Borisism
- see also **ceaseless carnal activity**, **imperial good-time girls**, **mimetic genius**

Moutarde de Meaux

'Moutarde de Meaux – any kind of meat is more or less bearable with mustard.'

Desert Island Discs, BBC Radio 4, 4 November 2005.

His choice of luxury item on the show.

- Coarse ground mustard from Meaux, a town in Northern France; *Meldois*, the town's inhabitants, derives from Meldi, Latin name for the Gaulish tribe who occupied the area

Muff it

'We can muff it. Yes, of course we can muff it. We can flunk it. We can vote for this deal, thereby confirming the worst suspicions of the British public about the cynicism of the elite, or else we can get it right and seize the opportunities before us.'

House of Commons, 14 January 2019.

Denouncing Theresa May's Brexit deal.

- *verb* to muff it; to handle a situation badly. Covering into which hands can be thrust to keep warm; Old French *mofle* 'large mitten'; also slang for a woman's genitals
- see also **bottled Brexit**, **jot and tittle**, **lapidary**, **polish a turd**, **Precambrian**, **queynte**

Multiple-bosomed

'It is a sign of the decline of any great civilisation that its people begin to worship strange gods … We have a new divinity that commands the adoration of the governing classes, as nannying and multiple-bosomed as Diana of Ephesus. Her name is Phobia, and sacrifices are being made at her altar.'

Daily Telegraph, 7 October 2004.

On how health and safety rules put the public at risk.

- Diana of Ephesus, goddess of fertility; statues of Diana show her covered with breasts, denoting fertility; it has also been suggested that they represent bulls' testicles. Phobia, from Greek, 'fear'
- see also **dur-brained**, **encephalopathic**, **scabophobic**

Murrain

'It is time to stop treating the EU referendum result as if it were a plague of boils or a murrain on our cattle.'

Speaking at Conservative Party conference, 3 October 2017.

- *noun* plague, epidemic; from Latin *mori* 'to die'; Old French *morine* 'carcass, body of dead animal'
- see also **autarkic**, **boosterism**, **Bre-entry**, **Bremain**, **dikbil**, **gloomadon poppers**, **whey**

Mutton-headed old mugwump

'A mutton-headed old mugwump.'

The Sun, 4 May 2017.

Attack on Labour leader Jeremy Corbyn, claiming he was a threat to national security. (Asked to say sorry, Boris replied sarcastically: 'I apologise to mugwumps everywhere.')

- *noun* mugwump, old, aloof. Originates from Algonquian native American *mugquomp* 'great chief'; in the *Harry Potter* novels, Albus Dumbledore is 'Supreme Mugwump'; also referenced in Roald Dahl's *Charlie and the Great Glass Elevator* ('my dear old muddle-headed mugwump'). Mutton-headed, stupid

- see also **Caracas, Heisenberg, hempen, ignoratio elenchi, lachrymose**

N

Namby-pamby

'The namby-pamby, pussy-footing around of the spheroid fetishists...'

Speech at the Rugby World Cup draw, 3 December 2012.

On football.

- *adjective* lacking courage, weak, ineffectual; coined by eighteenth-century English poet Henry Carey to mock rival poet
- see also **banana-booted demigod**, **Spheroids**

Narghileh

'He would lie back on the pillows and in one hand manipulate the celestial narghileh ... his other arm gently looped around the exposed stomach of the first of his statutory seventy-two almond-eyed virgins.'

Seventy-Two Virgins, 2004.

- *noun* traditional water pipe from Turkey (the native land of Johnson's great-grandfather) used for smoking tobacco; also known as a hookah; from *nargil*, Persian for coconut, used to make pipes

- see also **Aryan bull pig, hubble-bubble pipe, hur, Johnny Turk, raisins, sharmoota**

Natural as sewage

'It is common ground among both right-wingers and left-wingers that racism ... in all civilisations ... is as natural as sewage. We all agree it is disgusting, a byproduct of humanity's imperfect evolution. The question is, what to do with the effluent?'

The *Guardian*, 21 February 2000.

On how racism occurs across all strata of society.

- Borisism
- see also **acculturated, burqa, dusky, half-caste, piss against the wall, puffing coolies**

Nec tali auxilio, nec defensoribus istis

'My hon. Friend raises the issue of the support of the former Prime Minister. I am tempted to say "Nec tali auxilio, nec defensoribus istis".'

House of Commons, 22 November 2016.

Rejecting the idea of Tony Blair campaigning to promote the UK after Brexit.

- From Latin, a slight misquote of a phrase coined by Roman poet Virgil, meaning 'not such aid nor such defenders does the time require'
- see also **Aegyptia coniunx, equo ne credite, Teucri, guff, soi-disant poet, whiffled**

Nel mezzo del cammin di nostra vita

'A lot of journalists, when they find themselves nel mezzo del cammin di nostra vita, *start to be afflicted by doubts.'*
Friends, Voters, Countrymen, 2001.

When journalists feel the need to do something more worthwhile.

* From Italian, 'in the middle of the journey of our life'
* see also **boondoggle, epiphytes, glow-worm transience, millennialist suicide cult, pshaw, suppressio veri and suggestio falsi, swankpot journalists**

Nephos

'Spliffs and cigarettes were produced, and soon the gathering had created a nice little nephos of polyaromatic hydrocarbons and benzopyrenes.'
Seventy-Two Virgins, 2004.

* *noun* Ancient Greek word for cloud
* see also **icing sugar, Inca mummy, most jiving party, narghileh, psychotropical effect**

Neronian

'Compared to the Dutch, who managed to stamp out the disease within weeks, MAFF seemed Neronian in its apathy.'
Friends, Voters, Countrymen, 2001.

Criticising the government's reaction to a foot-and-mouth epidemic.

- *adjective* Roman Emperor Nero (37 AD–68 AD), accused of 'fiddling while Rome burned'
- see also **biggest creep in history, pater patriae**

Newt-fancying hypocrites

'A bunch of Trotskyist, car-hating, Hugo Chávez-idolising, newt-fancying hypocrites and bendy-bus fetishists.'

Conservative Party spring forum, 3 March 2012.

Attacking Ken Livingstone, his predecessor as London Mayor – known for his love of newts and admiration of the Marxist ex-President of Venezuela Hugo Chávez.

- see also **broken-backed diplodocus, Châteauneuf-du-Pape cabal, namby-pamby**

Nibelung

'They were his Nibelung, his elves, the tinkling dwarves in the smithy of Hephaestus.'

The Churchill Factor, 2014.

On the debt Churchill owed to munitions workers in the Second World War.

- *noun* Germanic mythology; Scandinavian race of dwarfs, ruled by Nibelung, king of Nibelheim, land of mist; Hephaestus, Greek god of fire who made weapons for Olympus
- see also **Ambrosia, empyrian, numen, oompa-loompa, Phlegethontian fires**

Nilotic

'She felt her soul-sickness deepen and she turned to the

front and saw Dean with his afro hair and his proud, pale, almost Nilotic features.'

Seventy-Two Virgins, 2004.

- *adjective* relationship to the Nile river or region; from Latin via Greek *Neilōtikos*, from *Neilos* 'Nile'
- see also **dusky, half-caste**

Nobel Peace Prize

'If he can fix North Korea and the Iran nuclear deal, then I don't see why he's any less of a candidate for a Nobel Peace Prize than Barack Obama, who got it before he even did anything.'

Washington Post, 8 May 2018.

On Donald Trump.

- see also **crack-brained neocons, Mexican stand-off, orally extemporising, part-Kenyan ancestral dislike, progenitor, Sisyphean, stupefying ignorance, sword of Damocles, whinge-o-rama**

Non-turgor factor

'In the old days, she says, people from the village could barely spit it out when they came to discuss their penile non-turgor factor.'

Friends, Voters, Countrymen, 2001.

Chatting to a doctor in his Henley constituency about the huge demand for Viagra among local men.

- Borisism
- *noun* impotence; from Latin *turgidus* 'swollen', 'inflated'; *non-turgor*, the opposite, hence Viagra

- see also **donger, flaccidity, one-eyed trouser snake, phallocratic phallus**

Nostos

'The Greeks called it nostos, the moment of return, and nostalgia is technically the longing for what should be a joyful occasion, but often isn't, of course.'

Seventy-Two Virgins, 2004.

- *noun* Ancient Greek, 'homecoming'; in Homer's *Odyssey*, Odysseus's return after the Trojan War; 'nostalgia', longing for the past or home
- see also **Aegean, Aeschylus, Disraeli and Achilles, Homeric code**

Not on the table

'We are absolutely resolved that there will be no sale of the NHS, no privatisation. The NHS is not on the table in any way.'

Sky News, 27 November 2019.

Rejecting Labour claims that the NHS would be 'up for sale' in post-Brexit trade talks with the US.

- see also **dolts and serfs, parable of the toast, tattooed bottoms**

Numbskulls

'I have seen British troops training the Nigerian forces to defeat the numbskulls of Boko Haram.'

Speaking at Conservative Party conference, 3 October 2017.

On fighting terrorism in Africa.

- *noun* a stupid person; an insult dating back to the late seventeenth century. Boko Haram, Nigerian Islamic fundamentalist terror group

- see also **pathetic Islamofascists, scum**

Numen

'Churchill's prophetic numen.'

The Churchill Factor, 2014.

- *noun* spirit or divine presence; from Latin via Greek, *noumenon*, 'will of the gods'
- see also **anaphora, chiasmus, epiphenomena, funky Gibbon, megalopsychia, orotund, prophetic hare, selfish tosser, syllogism, transmogrifying, Zeus and Polyhymnia, zingers**

Obiter dicta

'We have a crisis in Yemen … a burgeoning crisis in Egypt … far more important than any obiter dicta you may have disinterred from thirty years of journalism.'

First press conference as Foreign Secretary, 19 July 2016.

Dismissing attempts to question him over past controversies.

- *noun* legal term, incidental remark by judge; obiter, from Latin, 'by the way'; dicta, plural of *dictum*, 'something that has been said'

- see also **minestrone of observations**

Octavian the cornflake

'Octavian was the cornflake that gets to the top of the packet.'

The Dream of Rome, 2006.

Octavian (27 BC–14 AD), also known as Augustus, first Emperor of the Roman Empire.

- Borisism

- see also **cornflakes, get Agrippa**, **midfield playmaker**, **Ready Brek glow**

Onanistic

'She would bend over him, bringing her breasts ever closer to his face, laughing low and praising him and dissolving all the onanistic wretchedness of his previous life.'

Seventy-Two Virgins, 2004.

- *adjective* masturbation; in the Old Testament, Onan defied an order from his father to impregnate his deceased brother's wife; Onan withdrew before his orgasm and ejaculated onto the ground
- see also **Boobtropolis, buxom as all get out, donger, engine of Onan, mega-titted, raisins, soutien-gorges, tits in a wringer, Tottometer, wankerer**

One-eyed trouser snake

'It does wonders for the one-eyed trouser snake, says my friend the Oxfordshire GP, motioning with her hand to show the effects of the pill.'

Friends, Voters, Countrymen, 2001.

Discussing Viagra with a local doctor in his Henley constituency.

- euphemism; bawdy term for penis
- see also **bag of ferrets, bra-fetishist, donger, flaccidity, non-turgor factor, phallocratic phallus**

Oompa-loompas

'It wasn't some supernatural agency that nicked your bike ... It wasn't oompa-loompas or fairies or bike elves. It was thieves.'

Have I Got Views For You, 2006.

- *noun* diminutive fictional factory workers; from Roald Dahl's 1964 children's book *Charlie and the Chocolate Factory*
- see also **Ambrosia, Nibelung**

Optimis parentibus

Seventy-Two Virgins, 2004.

Book dedication to his father, writer and politician Stanley, and mother, artist Charlotte.

- From Latin, meaning 'to the best parents'; Latin *parire* 'to bring forth', and alternatively *parere* 'to obey'; also found in Aristotle's principle work *Metaphysics*
- see also **megalopsychia**

Orally extemporising

'Unlike the current occupant of the White House, he has no difficulty in orally extemporising a series of grammatical English sentences, each containing a main verb.'

Daily Telegraph, 21 October 2008.

Comparing Barack Obama to George W. Bush.

- *verb* to orally extemporise; make a speech without preparation; from Latin *ex tempore* 'instantaneously'
- see also **buzzard squint, crack-brained neocons, dada-ist**

Orotund

'Long, orotund, bombastic Churchillian circumlocutions.'

The Churchill Factor, 2014.

- *adjective* (of a person's voice) resonant and imposing; from Latin *ore rotundo*, literally 'with round mouth' often used to mean 'well-rounded phrases'

- see also **anaphora, chiasmus, epiphenomena, numen, syllogism, zingers**

P

Painful plastic cuboids

'Every year, we go to the Windsor-based theme park, built to celebrate those little plastic cuboids that are so painful to tread on in bare feet.'

Daily Telegraph, 29 July 2004.

On annual family visits to Legoland in Windsor, Berkshire.

- Borisism
- *noun* Lego brick
- see also **Homo sovieticus, Lego**

Palestinian doxy

'Please ring the French ambassador with my compliments, and tell him that he and his Palestinian doxy are fully expected in Westminster Hall.'

Seventy-Two Virgins, 2004.

- *noun* doxy, sweetheart or prostitute; from Middle Dutch *docke* 'doll'
- see also **fantastic goer, fornicating, imperial good-time girls, Paris Hilton, poule de luxe, sharmoota, wenching**

Panathenaic frieze

'I congratulate [Director of the British Museum] Neil MacGregor on getting the Terracotta Army to London but when you compare those universal imperial henchmen with the Panathenaic frieze you can see why democracy and individualism got going in western Europe rather than in east Asia.'

Speech at the Royal Academy, 3 June 2008.

Arguing that the frieze on the Parthenon in Athens, built in the fifth century BC, is superior to China's uniform Terracotta Army, created more than 200 years later.

- *noun* marble sculpture on upper part of the Parthenon; from Greek *pan* 'all'; athenaic, relating to Athens
- see also **Sinophobia, trabeate and arcuate, vertiginously**

Panther

'I'm like a greased panther, a coiled spring, all that suppressed kinetic energy.'

Sky News, 3 May 2006.

Joking about taking part in a charity England v Germany football match. His un-panther like performance included barging head-first into a German player's stomach.

- Borisism
- see also **banana-booted demigod, Bothamesque, greased piglet, Hyrcanian tiger, midfield playmaker, namby-pamby**

Papua New Guinea chief killing

'For ten years we in the Tory Party have become used to

Papua New Guinea-style orgies of cannibalism and chief-killing.'

Daily Telegraph, 7 September 2006.

Comparing Conservative Party infighting to cannibalism in Papua New Guinea.

- Borisism
- see also **il sont passes, ces beaux jours, Tory tosser**

Parable of the toast

'It ought to be possible for a well-heeled journalist, who has been so improvident as to eat his wife's toast in the middle of the night, to pay for some more. We need to think about new ways of getting private money into the NHS.'

Speech to South Oxfordshire Conservatives, 2001.

On a visit to wife Marina in hospital which convinced him of the case for more private cash in the NHS.

- see also **dolts and serfs, ils sont passes, ces beaux jours, matricide, not on the table, tattooed bottoms**

Parenthetically

'I would point out parenthetically that NOx pollution has in fact fallen by 29 per cent under this Conservative government.'

House of Commons, 25 July 2019.

Answering Green Party complaint.

- *adverb* to put a remark in parentheses; from Greek *parénthesis* 'putting in beside'
- see also **Brahmaputra, hempen, Toutatis, vertiginously**

Paris Hilton

'She is the prototype of ... every woman who has overcome a pretty rackety background to achieve great things ... It is as though Paris Hilton had married the President of the United States – not quite so unthinkable these days.'

The Dream of Rome, 2006.

Describing the marriage of sexually liberated Theodora to Emperor Justinian.

- Paris Hilton, an American socialite and model who gained notoriety when a sex tape involving herself and her ex-boyfriend was leaked in 2003
- see also **fantastic goer, mimetic genius, Palestinian doxy, poule de luxe, star-struck booby, wenching**

Part-Kenyan ancestral dislike

'Some said it was a snub to Britain. Some said it was a symbol of the part-Kenyan President's ancestral dislike of the British empire.'

The Sun, 22 April 2016.

Johnson's reaction to reports that Barack Obama had removed a bust of Churchill from the White House. Obama's father was born in Kenya in 1936, when it was still part of the British Empire.

- see also **flag-waving piccaninnies, Nobel Peace Prize, orally extemporising**

Pater patriae

'He calculates ... that he will appear to the goggling

*populace as a pater patriae, a reverse Cincinnatus who left
his desk in Whitehall to sort out the crisis on the farm.'*
Daily Telegraph, 3 April 2001.

Mocking Tony Blair's decision to postpone the 2001 election because of the foot-and-mouth disease crisis.

- *noun* Latin, father of the country, literally 'father of the fatherland';
  honour conferred by Roman Senate on Cicero, Julius Caesar and
  Augustus. Cincinnatus was a Roman statesmen who left his farm
  to save Rome from attack
- see also **Cincinnatus, Führerprinzip, get Agrippa, Neronian,
  vanilla nothingness, whiffled**

Pathetic Islamofascists

*'He found himself staring irresistibly at [her] … in her low
cut top. He felt the surge of fundamentalist rage that in-
spires the pathetic Islamofascistic male.'*
Seventy-Two Virgins, 2004

Johnson's theory that sexual frustration is a factor in Islamic fundamentalist terrorism.

- Islamofascism, the notion that Islamic fundamentalism is a political ideology not a religion, comparable to totalitarianism or
  fascism, prepared to use violence and bullying to impose its beliefs
- see also **acculturated, dirndl, ebullition, hur, numbskulls, scum,
  Taliban chappies, towelhead nutters, Wahhabi lust**

Pax vobiscum!

'Pax vobiscum! Hey, hey, it's Thanksgiving! Peace!'
Boris: The Rise of Boris Johnson, 2006.

Acting as peacemaker when *Spectator* publisher Kimberly Fortier clashed with writer Rod Liddle over smoking in the office.

- From Latin, 'peace be with you', salutation used in Catholic mass
- see also **militia amoris, pat on bottom**

Pegged

"'What do you mean, pegged them?" "Shot their mother-fucking asses.'"

Seventy-Two Virgins, 2004.

Conversation between two characters.

- Slang for anal sex performed by a woman on a man with a sex toy
- see also **medieval on their ass, Mexican stand-off, stuffed**

Penumbra

'We are going to leave the penumbra of European legislation.'

House of Commons, 18 October 2016.

- *noun* a peripheral area or group; from Latin *paene* 'almost', *umbra* 'shadow'
- see also **Bre-entry, Brexchosis, go whistle, umbilicus**

Pericles

'Round of applause, please, for Pericles.'

Speaking at a charity event to fund Latin teaching in schools, 18 September 2014.

He produced a bust of Pericles to be auctioned off.

- Borisism

- Pericles (c. 495 BC–429 BC), Greek orator and statesman; Johnson has a bust of him in his No. 10 study
- see also **dash of Dawson, dolichocephalic**

Phallocratic phallus

'To achieve more notches on my phallocratic phallus.'
Stated teenage ambition in the Eton 'leavers' book'.

- *adjective* masculine dominance; from Latin *phallus* 'penis', via Greek, *phallos*; Greek *kratos* 'power'
- see also **bag of ferrets, bra-fetishist, ceaseless carnal sex, donger, fantastic goer, non-turgor factor, satyriasis, shagged**

Pharaonic Hezzapolis

'Hezza may have had his vast pile, pillared, porticoed, pedimented, with an arboretum more stuffed with species than the rainforest. But the pharaonic Hezzapolis was to be found some way to the north of the constituency.'
Friends, Voters, Countrymen, 2001.

On his predecessor as Henley MP Michael Heseltine's country estate in Northamptonshire.

- *adjective* magnitude of a pharaoh in Ancient Egypt; Hezza is Heseltine's nickname
- see also **chunderous, entasis, matricide, Simba**

Phenotype

'The phenotype of Thatcherism is preserved in the genes of Blair.'
1997.

- *noun* characteristics or actions resulting from interaction between genetic disposition and the environment; from Greek *phainein* 'to show', *typos* 'type'
- see also **acnoid, Ambrosia, drag artistry, flinty, Führerprinzip, guff**

Phlegethontian fires

'It is appropriate, of course, that we are here in Telford, because here more than 200 years ago the Phlegethontian fires created the first industrial revolution.'

Conservative manifesto launch, 4 November 2019.

- *adjective* scaldingly hot; from Greek mythology, the river Phlegethon or Pyriphlegethon was a 'stream of fire'; described in Dante's *Inferno* as a river of blood that boils souls
- See also **empyrean, Nibelung**

Pikeys

'There were pikeys with whippets and Sloanes with toe-rings. Here was a dreadlocked black man flogging the Socialist Worker.'

Seventy-Two Virgins, 2004.

Describing a protest march in London.

- *noun* offensive term for member of the traveller community or working class; from 'pike', which meant 'highway' in the sixteenth century; or possibly Old English *pikka* 'peck', 'pick' or 'steal'
- see also **chavs**

Pilgrim of penitence

'I went on this pilgrim of penitence to Liverpool … to

*apologise for the factual error related to the number of
casualties at Hillsborough.'*

Desert Island Discs, BBC Radio 4, 4 November 2005.

On his visit to Liverpool after he was accused of smearing
the city in a *Spectator* article about the 1989 Hillsborough
football stadium disaster in which ninety-six fans died.

- Fourth-century Christian penitence movement; those who confessed serious sins went on pilgrimages to the Holy Land
- see also **ker-splonked**, **mayoral culpa**

Pindaric

*'We have not only revived the ancient cult of near-nudity
in the beach volleyball. The park also boasts … an ode to
the Games in Pindaric Greek.'*

Daily Telegraph, 6 August 2012.

Describing the 2012 London Olympics.

- Poetry by Pindar (518 BC–438 BC), celebrating a chariot victory by
  Queen Berenice at the Nemean Games in Ancient Greece
- See also **eudaimonia**, **gobsmacked**, **switcheroo**, **wet otters**

Pin-goaded stallion

*'The taxi driver … could barely look at me as he flung the
change through the window, and went off like a pin-goaded
stallion, almost running over my toe.'*

Friends, Voters, Countrymen, 2001.

- Borisism
- *noun* stallion, a horse; to pin-goad, to drive an animal with a
  spiked stick

- see also **Italian stallion, stung in the bum**

Pink-eyed terminators

'AI – what will it mean? Helpful robots washing and caring for an ageing population? Or pink-eyed terminators sent back from the future to cull the human race?'

Speech to the UN General Assembly in New York, 24 September 2014.

On the challenge of artificial intelligence (AI).

- Borisism
- Science fiction film series and eponymous cyborg *The Terminator*, starring Arnold Schwarzenegger; from Latin *terminus* 'end'
- see also **condom stuffed with walnuts, monosyllabic Austrian cyborg**

Piss against the wall

'Where primary immigration is on a large scale, there is only the vaguest sense of belonging. There seems no reason to behave respectfully towards the little old woman coming out of the Post Office if you feel she belongs to a culture alien from your own ... Why not piss against the wall if you feel it is not really your wall, but part of a foreign country.'

8 December 2000.

Linking lawlessness to immigration.

- *idiom* to urinate against a wall, showing disrespect; from Old French word *pissier*, meaning 'to urinate'
- see also **acculturated, burqa, Kulturkampf, piss-heads, re-Britannification, syncretic, xenophobe**

Piss-heads

'Out of the parking lot lurched the terrorists, up past the Red Lion pub, whence a couple of piss-heads surveyed them apathetically.'

Seventy-Two Virgins, 2004.

- *noun* colloquialism for people that are drunk
- see also **feckless, hogwhimpering, Jackson Pollocked, Maenads, piss against the wall**

Platitudinous Pooters

'In his speech, his dress, his bandanas, his face-lifts, his ludicrous 1950s cruise-ship sexism, he is a standing reproach to the parade of platitudinous Pooters that pass across the stage of international diplomacy.'

Daily Telegraph, 6 March 2006.

In praise of colourful Italian President Silvio Berlusconi.

- *noun* Pooter, slang for someone who is self-important and dull; Charles Pooter, main character in 1892 novel *Diary of a Nobody*. Platitude, statement used too often to have meaning, from French *plat* 'flat'
- see also **Führerprinzip, jut-jawed and jackbooted**

Plutocratic sneer

'I took in the ludicrously arrogant Darth Vader-style snout. What was it saying, with the plutocratic sneer of that gleaming grille? It was saying: " ... Make way for Murano!"'

Life in the Fast Lane, 2007.

On driving a Nissan Murano.

- *adjective* government by the wealthy; from Greek *ploutos* 'wealth', *kratos* 'power'
- see also **ponces and pseuds**

Po-faced

'Po-faced, pompous, prudish, pedantic, they are simultaneously money-grubbing and obscenely profligate.'
Have I Got Views For You, 2006.
Attacking Tony Blair's government.

- Borisism
- *adjective* humourless and disapproving; possibly abbreviated from poker-faced
- see also **Archaiser, buttock exposure, Caligula gleam, Gordonomics, guff, whiffle**

Polish a turd

'Anyone defending the proposal will find it like trying to polish a turd. Luckily, we have some expert turd-polishers in this government.'
6 July 2018.
His attack on Prime Minister Theresa May's Brexit deal at a Chequers summit that preceded his resignation as Foreign Secretary.

- *idiom* to make something unpleasant more pleasant than it really is; from Old English *tord* 'piece of dung'
- see also **bottled Brexit, fungible, jot and tittle, muff it, murrain, Precambrian, simulacrum**

Ponces and pseuds

'I thought Range Rovers were for posers, ponces and pseuds. "What's the difference between a hedgehog and a Range Rover?" someone asked me when I was ten ... "With a Range Rover, the pricks are all on the inside."'

Life in the Fast Lane, 2007.

- *noun* ponce, pimp; pseud, someone who is pretentious, from Greek *pseudes* 'false, lying'
- see also **Plutocratic sneer**

Popty-ping

'Pop it in the popty-ping.'

Interview with Welsh journalist Guto Hari, 10 December 2019.

Describing his Brexit deal as a meal ready to go in the microwave.

- *noun* from Welsh *popty-ping* 'microwave oven'
- see also **diolch yn fawr**, **pysgod a sglodion**

Postcoital detumescence

'Slowly the foot came off the throttle like some postcoital detumescence.'

Life in the Fast Lane, 2007.

On slowing down.

- *noun* when the penis deflates after sexual intercourse; postcoital, Latin *post* 'after', *coitus*, sexual intercourse; detumescense, Latin *de* 'down, away', *tumescere* 'swell'
- see also **fully extended bonk**, **gynaecomorphised**, **Italian stallion**, **non-turgor factor**

Post hoc ergo propter hoc

'[Brexit] is about continuing the revolution in tastes and styles … that has taken place in this country not so much because of our EU membership – that is to commit the fallacy known in the FCO as post hoc ergo propter hoc – but as a result of our history and global links.'

14 February 2018.

Challenging the Foreign Office view that modern Britain was shaped more by the EU than its own national history.

- From Latin, 'after this, therefore because of this'
- see also **fungible**, **homo foederalis**

Potemkin objects

'We drivers must accept that these cameras are no longer Potemkin objects, as they seemed to be for the first few years, empty scarecrows with no film in them.'

Daily Telegraph, 20 May 2004.

On taking up cycling after a series of speeding fines.

- *noun* speed cameras that are no longer fake; 'Potemkin villages' were built by Prince Potemkin, eighteenth-century Russian statesman and lover of Catherine the Great, to disguise the true extent of poverty from her when she toured Russia
- see also **limbless mendicants**

Poule de luxe

'I twanged the Winged Victory … as one might twang a tentative bra strap. Was there any of us who would not be affected by the beauty of the burred walnut fascia, the

white leather seats as soft as the purse of some Saudi poule de luxe?'

Life in the Fast Lane, 2007.

On driving a Rolls-Royce.

- *noun* high-class hooker; French *poule* 'hen', slang for prostitute; poule de luxe, expensive prostitute
- see also **Boobtropolis, buxom as all get out, fantastic goer, fornicating, fully extended bonk, Palestinian doxy, soutien-gorges**

Pouty sadistic nurse

'She's got dyed blonde hair and pouty lips, and a steely blue stare, like a sadistic nurse in a mental hospital.'

Daily Telegraph, 1 November 2007.

Lampooning Hilary Clinton.

- Borisism
- see also **pretzel-words, scandal in the wind, star-struck booby**

Power squiggles

'They took out their fountain pens and left their power squiggles on the vellum of history.'

The Dream of Rome, 2006.

The 2004 signing of the EU constitution.

- Borisism
- *noun* leaders' signatures
- see also **dithyramb, fungible, Procrustean squeezing, vinegarish**

Praeteritio

'By way of praeteritio, I want to deal with a solution we

will certainly not employ, agreeable though it might be for red-faced colonels in the Home Counties ... there simply will not be ... a military solution.'
Westminster Hall debate, 15 July 2003.

On why Britain could not use force to topple Robert Mugabe in Zimbabwe.

- *noun* a rhetorical device of calling attention to an idea or argument that is not to be considered; from Latin, 'omission', 'passing over'

- see also **anaphora, chiasmus**

Prangmeister

'I see idiots and crash-artists and prangmeisters and fools who change nappies on the hard shoulder.'
Daily Telegraph, 20 May 2004.

- Borism

- Conflating 'prang', slang for car crash, with German *meister* 'master'

- see also **Testadicazzo**

Precambrian

'In one of the most protoplasmic displays of invertebracy since the Precambrian epoch, this government has decided not to fulfil the mandate of the people.'
Daily Telegraph, 26 March 2019.

On Theresa May's decision to delay the UK's departure from the EU.

- *noun* earliest part of Earth's history when hard-shelled creatures first become prevalent

- see also **Bremain, gelatinous, jot and tittle, lapidary, muff it, polish a turd, protoplasmic invertebrate jellies, simulacrum**

Prelapsarian

'He described a wonderful prelapsarian world in which he and his children would camp under the stars, with nothing but mosquito nets, or dive to retrieve fishing lures from croc-infested pools.'

Daily Telegraph, 30 August 2010.

On a trip to Africa.

- *adjective* literary term for 'before the fall of man'; from English 'pre', 'before', Latin *lapus*, from *labi* 'to fall'
- see also **charismatic megafauna, impis, Tsavo**

Pretzel-words

'Yesterday, in a feat of Clintonian pretzel-words, he told us that, in order to understand this flagrant inconsistency, we had to look at the "totality" of his words, because he also said that he did not authorise the "leaking" of the name.'

Daily Telegraph, 8 January 2004.

Rejecting Tony Blair's denial of blame over the circumstances leading to the suicide of MoD scientist Dr David Kelly.

- Borisism
- Words tied up in knots, like a pretzel, a German pastry baked in a knot-like shape
- see also **guff, scandal in the wind, schlockiest bonkbuster, suppressio veri and suggestio falsi, whiffled, witchetty grub**

Procrustean squeezing

'The reason I became a sceptic about integration was that it continually involved a Procrustean squeezing or chopping of national interests.'

Have I Got Views For You, 2006.

On EU integration.

- *adjective* enforcing uniformity or conformity without regard to individuality; from Greek mythology, Procrustes, who cut off people's legs or stretched them on a rack to force them to fit into an iron bed
- see also **fungible**, **give a monkey's**, **homo foederalis**, **vinegarish**

Progenitor

'I cannot say who was the exact progenitor of the excellent idea to accord an invitation to the President to come on a state visit, but the invitation has been issued.'

House of Commons, 21 February 2017.

Claiming credit for Donald Trump's state visit to the UK.

- *noun* a person or thing from which an idea or being is descended; from Latin, 'ancestor', 'founder of a family', from the verb *progignere, pro-* 'forward', *gignere* 'produce'
- see also **Nobel Peace Prize**, **stupefying ignorance**, **whinge-o-rama**

Pro having cake and pro eating it

'[Britain's EU stance should be] like our policy on cake – pro having it and pro eating it.'

2016.

Claiming it is possible to both leave the EU and retain good links with it.

- Borisism
- Sixteenth-century proverb 'you cannot have your cake and eat it' turned on its head. Original version, meaning 'you can't have it both ways', first recorded in letter from Duke of Norfolk to Thomas Cromwell, Henry VIII's chief minister
- see also **Bre-entry**, **Bremain**, **murrain**

Prometheus

'When Prometheus brought fire to mankind ... Zeus punished him by chaining him to a tartarean crag while his liver was pecked out by an eagle. Every time his liver regrew the eagle came back and pecked it again. This went on for ever – a bit like Brexit...'

Speech to the UN General Assembly in New York, 24 September 2019.

On the three-year parliamentary deadlock on Brexit.

- Greek mythology; Prometheus stole fire from Zeus and gave it to the mortals, for which he was eternally punished
- see also **Brexchosis**, **muff it**, **polish a turd**, **Zeus and Polyhymnia**

Prophetic hare

'[Boudica] had a bosom so big that she was capable of using it to conceal her prophetic hare, an animal she would whisk out at the end of her bellicose speeches, and invoke, depending on whether it ran left or right, to foretell the outcome of battle.'

The Spirit of London, 2012.

- Boudica (died c. 60 or 61 AD), queen of Iceni tribe of Britons who fought the Romans

- see also **buxom as all get out, mega-titted, multiple-bosomed, numen**

Prostatic indignities
'[He] had spent the last few minutes sitting in the back while rubber-gloved officers subjected the taxi to prostatic indignities.'
Seventy-Two Virgins, 2004.
- *adjective* examination of the prostate
- see also **up the Arcelor**

Protoplasmic invertebrate jellies
'Great, supine, protoplasmic, invertebrate jellies!'
Speaking to the London Assembly, 25 February 2013.
Attacking opposition party members of the London Assembly as mayor.
- Borisism
- *noun* implying spinelessness i.e. cowardice, weakness
- see also **gelatinous, protozoan**

Protozoan
'A young lady had asked him about abortion, and his answer had been protozoan in its invertebracy.'
Seventy-Two Virgins, 2004.
- *adjective* implying someone has acted without a backbone and therefore without courage; *noun* single-celled microscopic animal, such as an amoeba
- see also **gelatinous, protoplasmic invertebrate jellies, scuzzy**

Prozac-munching morons

'It is true that I may have written a few columns accusing Labour backbenchers of being a bunch of Prozac-munching morons.'

Friends, Voters, Countrymen, 2001.

- *noun* Prozac, anti-depressant drug

Pshaw

'Pshaw, said Johnson. There was one reason writers were writers: the pleasure that goes with a repetition of their own names … "like a monarch in disguise", cocking a pathetic ear to hear what the world is making of his latest effort – the crushing reality is no one is even talking about the thing.'

The Spirit of London, 2012.

Quoting eighteenth-century writer Samuel Johnson on the vanity and irrelevance of journalists.

- Borisism
- Eighteenth-century expression of contempt or impatience
- see also **epiphytes, glow-worm transience, nel mezzo del cammin di nostra vita, snooks, suppressio veri and suggestio falsi, swankpot journalists, tits in a wringer**

Psychotropical effect

'I tried it at university and I remember it vividly … It achieved no pharmacological, psychotropical or any other effect on me whatsoever.'

GQ, July 2007.

On being asked by Piers Morgan if he had tried cocaine.

- *verb* mind changing; from Greek *psycho* 'mind', *tropos* 'turning', hence 'turn the mind'
- see also **icing sugar, Inca mummy, most jiving party, nephos**

Pudding basin

'He has a big protuberant Roman snout, and thick booby-ish lips, and a pudding basin haircut.'
The Dream of Rome, 2006.

On Publius Quinctilius Varus (46 BC–9 AD), a Roman general who committed suicide after being defeated by Germanic tribes led by Arminius in the Battle of Teuto-burg Forest in 15 AD.

- *noun* crude haircut achieved by putting a bowl on someone's head and cutting around the edge
- see also **Cannae, flobbery, Pyrrhic, Rolf Harris didgeridoos, supercilious sibilance**

Puffed-up popinjay

'We will not allow US–UK relations to be endangered by some puffed-up pompous popinjay in City Hall.'
Twitter, 12 January 2018.

Attacking London Labour Mayor Sadiq Khan, a prominent critic of Donald Trump.

- *noun* a vain or conceited person; popinjay, archaic term for parrot, potentially derived from the Old French/Dutch *papegai* 'parrot'
- see also **crack-brained neocons, guff, stupefying ignorance, whinge-o-rama**

Puffing coolies

'Within minutes they were toting Sir Richard's oeuvre like puffing coolies.'

Daily Telegraph, 16 February 1996.

On the reaction of MPs to the Scott Report, commissioned by John Major's government to investigate the arms-to-Iraq scandal involving Tory minister Alan Clark.

- *noun* coolies, offensive term for unskilled Chinese or Indian labourers; from Hindi *quli* 'slave'
- see also **dusky, Hottentot, Latinate evasion, watermelon smiles**

Pullulate

'Smart cities will pullulate with sensors, all joined together by the "internet of things", bollards communing invisibly with lamp posts.'

Speech to the UN General Assembly in New York, 24 September 2019.

- *verb* to pullulate; to breed or spread prolifically or rapidly; from the Latin word *pullulatus*, meaning 'put forth', 'grow', 'sprout'
- see also **dystopian fantasy, engine of Onan, jabberama, Twitter-borne transphobes**

Punctilious

'The government is absolutely punctilious in wanting to meet our friends more than halfway.'

Foreign Office, London, 7 December 2017.

Implying that Britain was being more than reasonable about its Brexit 'divorce bill'.

- *adjective* showing great attention to detail or correct behaviour; from Italian *puntiglio* 'point of honour'; Latin *punctum* 'point'
- see also **autarkic, Bre-entry**

Pushmi-pullyu

'He resembles a … pushmi-pullyu facing in both directions at once and unable to decide for either. His policy on cake is neither having it nor eating it.'

House of Commons, 14 October 2019.

On Jeremy Corbyn's Brexit stance.

- *noun* someone who behaves in a contradictory manner; double-headed creature from Hugh Lofting's *Doctor Dolittle* children's books
- see also **Caracas, Heisenberg, hempen, ignoratio elenchi, lach-rymose, mutton-headed old mugwump, pro having cake and pro eating it**

Pusillanimously

'The Belgian king had pusillanimously run up the white flag at midnight.'

The Churchill Factor, 2014.

- *adverb* lack of courage; from Latin *pusillanimis* 'having little cour-age', 'small mind'
- see also **antepartum, dikbil, Little Britons, weevilled**

Pyrrhic

'It may be true that after months of barbaric bombing Bashar

al-Assad and his Russian and Iranian sponsors are on the
point of capturing Aleppo ... But it will be a Pyrrhic victory.'
Speech in Bahrain, 9 December 2016.
On the conflict in Syria.

- *adjective* victory won at too great a cost; King Pyrrhus of Epirus
  suffered such heavy losses in defeating the Romans at the Battle of
  Heraclea in 280 BC and the Battle of Asculum in 279 BC that he
  said another such victory would undo him

- see also **Cannae, Dobby, media ectoplasm, pudding basin, supercilious sibilance**

Pysgod a sglodion

*'I had learnt the Welsh language, to the point where I could
order a pint of beer or fish and chips,* pysgod a sglodion.'
Friends, Voters, Countrymen, 2001.

- Welsh for 'fish and chips'
- see also **diolch yn fawr, popty-ping**

Q

Quangocrat

'He was fluent, amiable, and highly intelligent. I expect he'll be on all kinds of boards, a quangocrat, a peer.'

Friends, Voters, Countrymen, 2001.

- Borisism
- Morphing 'bureaucrat', from French *bureau* 'desk' or 'office', Greek *kratos* 'rule' or 'power', with 'quango', from the acronym for a quasi-autonomous non-governmental organisation, QUANGO
- see also **adoptocrat**

Queynte

'The pleasure and magic ... was to take a sensible Latinate word and find a raunchy English pun. Take the word queynte, *from the Latin* cognitus, *meaning clever or learned, and which happens to be a variant spelling for an Anglo-Saxon four-letter-word that looks like a Danish king.'*

The Spirit of London, 2012.

On the mischievous genius of Geoffrey Chaucer's use of

the uniquely rich Germanic and Romantic roots of the English language in 'The Miller's Tale'.

- From Latin *cognitus* 'clever'; Anglo-Saxon swear word for intimate part of woman's body (clue: King Cnut)
- see also **blubbering ninny, donger, gynaecomorphised, Latinate evasion, muff it, vaginal endearment**

Quislings

'These would-be quislings were not alone.'
The Churchill Factor, 2014.
Describing members of the British establishment who wanted to do a deal with Hitler.

- *noun* traitor who collaborates with an enemy force occupying their country; from Norwegian Vidkun Quisling, Prime Minister of Norway's pro-Nazi puppet government
- see also **pusillanimously, Stilton-eating surrender monkeys, weevilled**

R

Raging homunculus

'I closed my eyes, sank back on the bubblegummed seat, and tried to control the raging homunculus within.'

Daily Telegraph, 3 July 2003.

Describing his frustration at being stuck on a train.

- *noun* little man; diminutive of Latin *homo* 'man'
- see also **crapshoot**

Raisins

"'Black-eyed ones might not mean seventy-two virgin girls … they now think it's a mistranslation, and it really means … raisins," said the President. "You blow yourself up thinking you're going to get seventy-two black-eyed virgins, and instead you get seventy-two raisins. Kind of makes a difference."'

Seventy-Two Virgins, 2004.

- Borisism
- see also **hur, nargileh, onanistic, sharmoota, Wahhabi lust**

Raw prawn

'They say the UK is like some poor wriggling crustacean about to be deprived of its shell. I say – don't come the raw prawn with me.'

Speech in Sydney, 27 July 2017.

Denying that leaving the EU would leave the UK exposed.

- Borisism
- *idiom* Australian, 'don't pull one over on me'; Second World War military slang, raw prawn, hard to swallow
- see also **autarkic**, **Bremain**, **chunderous**, **daks**, **lobster**, **murrain**, **whey**, **witchetty grub**

Ready Brek glow

'Everyone was suffused with a kind of Ready Brek glow of happiness and from then on it was as if nothing could go wrong.'

Conservative Party conference, 9 October 2012.

On the London Olympics.

- Borisism
- *noun* joyful; from 'get up and glow', a 1980s advertising slogan for Ready Brek, an oat-based cereal, featuring children going to school with a superimposed glow
- see also **cornflakes**, **eudaimonia**, **gobsmacked**, **Octavian the cornflake**, **switcheroo**, **vaginal endearment**

Re-Britannification

'It is a cultural calamity that will take decades to reverse, and we must begin now with … the re-Britannification of Britain.'

Daily Telegraph, 14 July 2005.

On how to stop British-born suicide bombers by re-establishing British values among British-born Muslims.

- Borisism
- *Britannia*, Roman name for Britain, later personified as goddess armed with trident and shield
- see also **acculturated, Britannia's ass, burqa, Kulturkampf, piss against the wall, syncretic, xenophobe**

Reincarnated as an olive

'My chances of being PM are about as good as the chances of finding Elvis on Mars, or my being reincarnated as an olive.'

The Independent, 2004.

Playing down his political ambition.

- Borisism
- Reincarnated, reborn in another body; from Latin *carnis* 'flesh'; literally 're-enter the flesh'
- see also **Achilles and Disraeli, Cincinnatus, cursus honorum**

Revanchist

'A revanchist Russia and the Islamist terror originating in ungoverned spaces in the Middle East and north Africa that have hideous consequences in our streets.'

Interview in *The Guardian*, 19 September 2017.

On his challenges as Foreign Secretary.

- *noun* seeking to retaliate, recover lost territory; from French *revanche* 'revenge'
- see also **acculturated, Dobby, Kulturkampf, media ectoplasm**

Rictus of amazement

'Let us keep the audience in a rictus of amazement, eyes popping, hands to mouth in suppressed gasps.'

Friends, Voters, Countrymen, 2001.

On retaining people's attention during a speech.

- *noun* fixed grimace or grin, open-mouthed expression; from Latin *rictus* 'open-mouthed'
- see also **ecstasy of Widdecombe, gibbering rictus, Hottentot**

Rocketing pheasant

'I see the hon. and learned Gentleman rise from his seat like a rocketing pheasant … Well, like a very slowly rocketing pheasant.'

House of Commons, 4 October 2006.

Addressing bon viveur, barrister and Labour MP Bob Marshall-Andrews.

- Borisism
- *noun* large gamebird launching into the sky at pace
- see also **gift of death**

Rolf Harris didgeridoos

'The Germanic tribesman were in the habit of emitting a blood-curdling noise called the Baritus … like a chorus of Rolf Harris didgeridoos.'

The Dream of Rome, 2006.

- *noun* didgeridoo, wind instrument of Aboriginal Australians; made famous by Australian entertainer Rolf Harris (jailed in 2014 for sexually assaulting young girls). *Baritus*, Germanic war cry used in battle against Romans

- see also **chunderous, pudding basin, raw prawns**

Roman swanking

'It was a classic piece of Roman swanking, and likely to be accompanied by huge public interest.'
The Dream of Rome, 2006.
Roman showing-off.

- *verb* to swank; display of wealth, knowledge, or achievements to impress others; possibly from German *sweng* 'to swing'
- see also **swankpot journalists**

Rumbustious

'Fat, jolly, high-living, rumbustious.'
The Churchill Factor, 2014.
On Churchill.

- *adjective* boisterous, unruly; from Old English, combination of *rum* 'good, fine', and robust
- see also **anaphora, chiasmus, epiphenomena, funky Gibbon, Gibbonian, megalopsychia, numen, runty kid, selfish tosser, syllogism, transmogrifying**

Runty kid

'Gingery young Churchill was a pretty runty sort of kid.'
The Churchill Factor, 2014.
On schoolboy Churchill's lack of sporting or academic prowess.

- *adjective* runt, smallest of a litter of pigs
- see also **funky Gibbon, Gibbonian, megalopsychia, numen, rumbustious, world king**

S

Sac de vomissement
'Churchill had been cited so often that the French Ambassador was calling for le sac de vomissement.'
Seventy-Two Virgins, 2004.

- Borisism
- *noun* 'sick bag'; from French *sac* 'bag', *vomi* 'sick'
- see also **chunderous, donnez-moi un break, Jackson Pollocked**

Sandpapered
'I mildly sandpapered something somebody said.'
The Andrew Marr Show, BBC One, 4 March 2013.
On making up a quote about Edward II for a *Times* article in 1988, which led to him being sacked as a trainee.

- Borisism
- *verb* to sandpaper; smooth over
- see also **inverted pyramid of piffle, Latinate evasion, Scarface, suppressio veri and suggestio falsi**

Sassenach

'Och aye, it's a land of milk and honey they're building up there in Scotland, laddie. They'll nae be doing with your horrid Anglo-Saxon devil-take-the-hindmost approach. No, they're just more socialist than us sour-mouthed Sassenachs.'

Daily Telegraph, 1 February 2001.

On Labour's domination of Scotland (before the rise of the Scottish Nationalists).

- *noun* derogatory Scottish term for an English person; from Scottish Gaelic *sasunnach* 'Saxon'

- see also **Aeneas MacTavish**, **monomanaical**

Satyriasis

'He may have a bad case of satyriasis … but it doesn't add up to harassment of women. The same argument is used in Britain and needs to be tackled head-on. Extra-marital sex is said to be of political relevance … because it exposes a basic treacherousness. Oh really? It is nothing to do with us. Politics is trivialized and turned into hell for so many of its practioners.'

Daily Telegraph, 28 January 1998.

Defending Bill Clinton over the Monica Lewinsky sex scandal – and all politicians caught up in sex scandals.

- *noun* uncontrollable sex drive; in Greek mythology, Satyr is part man, part beast with a large phallus

- see also **bra-fetishist, donger, epic poem, feline prowlings, flaccidity, non-turgor factor, one-eyed trouser snake, phallocratic phallus, scandal in the wind**

Scabophobic

'The scabophobic measures we have taken to protect our children have had consequences we could not have intended.'
Daily Telegraph, 13 December 2007.

On overzealous attempts to protect children.

- Borisism
- *adjective* excessive measures to stop children suffering cuts and bruises; from 'scab' and Greek *phobic* 'fear'
- see also **dur-brained, encephalopathic, splutterissimo**

Scandal in the wind

'... Bill Clinton and Tony Blair stood forth as the two buddies. Achilles and Patroclus. Castor and Pollux. Never mind Elton, there was scandal in the wind.'
Daily Telegraph, 7 February 1998.

On Tony Blair's staunch defence of Bill Clinton at a White House event with Elton John at the height of the Monica Lewinsky scandal.

- Borisism
- 'Candle in the Wind', Elton John song. The relationship between Achilles and Patroclus features in the Trojan War in Homer's *Iliad*; in some versions, they were lovers. Castor and Pollux, twin half-brothers in Greek and Roman mythology
- see also **Aeschylus, equo ne credite, Teucri, Homeric code, hypothalamus, Inca mummy, Kylie's rear, pouty sadistic nurse, pretzel-words, satyriasis, star-struck booby**

Scansion

'We're going to have a national poetry Olympiad to restore rhyme and scansion. There will be some sort of stoop of wine for the winning prize.'

The Guardian, May 2004.

On being appointed Conservative shadow Arts spokesman.

- *noun* scanning a line of verse in a poem to determine its rhythm; short and long syllables in poetry; from Latin *scandere* 'climb'; stoop, Old Norse *stoup* 'vessel'
- see also **epic poem, Spheroids, wankerer**

Scarface

'I try to tell the truth … It is Tony Montana in the film Scarface *who says: "I always tell the truth even when I lie."'*

The Observer, 19 October 2014.

Justifying his reputation for lack of truthfulness.

- Tony 'Scarface' Montana is a gangster played by Al Pacino in the 1983 film
- see also **inverted pyramid of piffle, Latinate evasion, Mexican stand-off, pegged, sandpapered, toad beneath the harrow**

Schindler

'The Oskar Schindler of the Upper House.'

27 November 1999.

Comparing Conservative Lord Cranborne, who saved the positions of ninety-two hereditary peers when Tony Blair reformed the House of Lords in 1999, to German industrialist Oskar Schindler, who saved the lives of 1,200 Jews during the Holocaust.

- Borisism
- see also **Kylie's rear**, **Stilton-eating surrender monkeys**

Schlockiest bonkbuster

'*Put down* The Da Vinci Code ... *Let Jilly Cooper turn yellow and wilt by the pool. I have before me a beach read more shocking than the schlockiest bonkbuster...*'

Daily Telegraph, 26 August 2004.

Describing the Butler Report into Tony Blair's use of intelligence surrounding Saddam Hussein's weapons of mass destruction in the run-up to the 2003 Iraq War.

- Borisism
- *adjective* schlockiest, from North American 'schlock', trashy goods; Yiddish *shlak* 'wretch', 'apoplectic stroke'. Bonkbuster, sexually explicit novel; bonk, English slang for sex
- see also **buttock exposure**, **Caligula gleam**, **crack-brained neocons**, **guff**, **pretzel-words**, **superannuated taramasalata**, **witchetty grub**

Schmoozathon

'*I congratulate the Prime Minister on the élan and success with which he has begun his pan-European schmoozathon in the chancelleries of Europe.*'

House of Commons, 1 June 2015.

On David Cameron's visits to EU leaders to try to win a better deal for the UK.

- Borisism

- schmoozing, from Yiddish *shmuesn*, 'to chat'; to chat in a persuasive manner, especially to gain favour; and *-athon*, marathon, prolonged
- see also **Bremain, demotic, Eurydice, girly swot, snore-athon, toad beneath the harrow**

Sclerotic

'Britain had been transformed from a sclerotic militant-ridden basket-case to a dynamic enterprise economy.'
Daily Telegraph, 16 November 2009.
On Britain's revival under Margaret Thatcher.

- *adjective* becoming rigid and unresponsive; losing the ability to adapt; from Latin *scleroticus* via Greek *skleros* 'hard'
- see also **Ambrosia, boosterism, execration, flinty, matricide**

Scrumple

'One man takes a look at my leaflet … Scrumple, scrumple.'
Friends, Voters, Countrymen, 2001.
Describing the lack of interest in election leaflets he was handing out in his Henley constituency.

- *verb* to scrumple; to crumple or screw up a piece of paper
- see also **chunderous, Simba, stumblebum**

Scum

'Let's find the scum who did this and wipe them off the face of the Earth.'
Have I Got Views For You, 2006.
On how to deal with terrorists responsible for the 9/11 attacks on the US.

- *noun* lowest form of human life; from German *schum* 'scum'
- see **also medieval on their ass, pathetic Islamofascists, Taliban chappies**

Scuzzy

'*He remembered a pro-abortion march he'd seen in London, and his feeling of disgust at these scuzzy rentamob characters screaming for the right to kill the unborn.*'

Seventy-Two Virgins, 2004.

- *adjective* dirty, unpleasant; blend of scummy and fuzzy
- see also **protozoan**

Scylla and Charybdis

'*We are between a rock and a hard place; the devil and the deep blue sea. We have on one side the Scylla of the backstop and on the other the Charybdis of infinite parliamentary delay.*'

Daily Telegraph, 26 March 2019.

On the parliamentary deadlock over the Northern Ireland Brexit 'backstop'.

- Being forced to choose between two similarly dangerous situations; from Greek mythology, two sea monsters at the entrance to the narrow Strait of Messina. Sailors who avoided one were caught by the other
- see also **backstop-ectomy, Brexchosis**

Seal-skin jockstrap

'*[Barbarians] clad in nothing but the kind of fur accessories*

you might find in a fetish shop – a seal-skin jockstrap, a rabbit-skin loincloth.'
The Dream of Rome, 2006.

- *noun* undergarment used to protect a man's genitals during sport. 'Bike jockey strap', made to protect cyclists on the cobblestone streets of Boston, US in 1870s
- see also **bra-fetishists, Châteauneuf-du-Pape cabal, namby-pamby, newt-fancying hypocrites, supercilious sibilance**

Selfish tosser

'When a friend was injured in the Omdurman campaign, he rolled up his sleeve and provided a skin graft himself – without anaesthetic. Was this the action of a selfish tosser?'
The Churchill Factor, 2014.

Rebutting the claim that Churchill was self-obsessed.

- *noun* crude way of calling someone egocentric; 'toss', slang for masturbating
- see also **epiphenomena, megalopsychia, numen, syllogism, Tory tosser, Zeus and Polyhymnia**

Semolina blob

'Hunting is crucial to Labour because it gives some contour to the semolina-like blob of Tony Blair's ideology.'
Daily Telegraph, 18 January 2001.

Arguing that Labour opposed hunting to make up for Tony Blair's lack of socialist – or other – principles.

- *noun* coarse wheat used to make pasta, and, mixed with milk, a creamy dessert; from Italian *semola* 'bran', via Latin *simila* 'flour'

- see also **cauls, gift of death, gralloched, guff, sexual yipping, Tiglath-Pileser, tweed-wearing atavism, vanilla nothingness**

Sexist fronde

'William Hague has correctly understood that if the Tories slide into a gay-bashing, wog-bashing, sexist fronde, they aren't history. They are biology. They are physics.'
Daily Telegraph, 10 October 1997.

On William Hague's calls for the Conservatives to be more socially progressive.

- Borism
- *noun* The Fronde, civil wars in France 1648–53; 'Fronde', sling, weapon used in the conflict. Gay-bashing, abuse of homosexuals. Wog-bashing, 'wog', from 'golliwog', black-faced minstrel character from children's fiction; racial slur
- see also **anti-aphrodisiacal properties, Boobtropolis, brafetishist, dolichocephalic, hippomonstrosesquippedaliophobia, Taliban chappies, tank-topped bumboys**

Sexpot adventuress

'When her first hotel burned down, she built another, and then went off to run a riotous establishment in Panama. She went prospecting for gold. She roasted and ate iguanas. She had a (possibly fictitious) encounter with Lola Montes, the noted sexpot and adventuress.'
The Spirit of London, 2012.

The exploits of Mary Seacole, the black British nurse who worked alongside Florence Nightingale in the Crimean War.

- Borisism
- Lola Montes, Irish-born beauty and dancer whose lovers included the King of Bavaria and, reputedly, Mary Seacole
- see also **fantastic goer, imperial good-time girls, lascivious matrons**

Sexually liberated

'In so far as this huge division in attitudes has appeared in what was a united Roman world, we must trace it to the Muslim invasions … Can you think of a single female figure in the Muslim world that was both sexually liberated and politically important? Neither can I.'

The Dream of Rome, 2006.

Arguing that after the Muslims conquered Constantinople the idea of a sexually liberated, powerful female such as Theodora, wife of Justinian, Roman Emperor of Byzantine, was unthinkable.

- see also **Aryan bull pig, fantastic goer, imperial good-time girls, Johnny Turk, lascivious matrons, Palestinian doxy, Paris Hilton, poule de luxe, Wahhabi lust**

Sexual yipping

'I can see it now, stepping high in the water, eyes rolling, tongue protruding, foaming, antlers streaming bracken and leaves like the hat of some demented old woman, and behind it the sexual, high-pitched yipping of the dogs.'

Lend Me Your Ears, 2003.

Describing the end of a stag hunt.

- *verb* to yip; a short, sharp cry or yelp
- see also **Brueghelian, cauls, gift of death, gralloched, Tiglath-Pileser, tweed-wearing atavism**

Shagged

'It was a long article by someone called Lucy Goodbody, in the [Guardian] G2 section, called "Breadline Britain". "I shagged her," said Paulie. "I shagged some reporter from the Guardian*."'*

Seventy-Two Virgins, 2004.

Boast by a character in the novel.

- *verb* slang for sex; from Old English *shag* 'waggle'
- see also **divine gift of lewdness, donger, fantastic goer, fornicating, phallocratic phallus, wenching**

Sharmoota

'It is a sharmoota. It is a whore.'

Seventy-Two Virgins, 2004.

- *verb* derogatory Arabic term; whore, bitch
- see also **bit of black, fantastic goer, Palestinian doxy, poule de luxe, wenching**

Shit-or-bust

'The shadow Education Secretary says that Labour's economic policy is ... "shit-or-bust"; I say it is both.'

4 September 2019.

Attacking a comment by Labour MP Angela Rayner.

- *noun* slang; high-risk, high-reward strategy
- see also **Gordonomics**

Simba

'There is a poignant moment in The Lion King *when Simba the cub realises he must succeed Mufasa, the bushy-maned king of the veld...'*

Friends, Voters, Countrymen, 2001.

Replacing Michael Heseltine as MP for Henley.

- Simba the lion cub succeeds his father, Mufasa, as leader of the pride in Disney's 1994 film *The Lion King*
- see also **chunderous, entasis, matricide, pharaonic Hezzapolis, scrumple, stumblebum**

Simulacrum

'No one voted for this type of Brexit. This is not Brexit, but a feeble simulacrum of national independence.'

House of Commons, 4 December 2018.

Setting out his opposition to Theresa May's Brexit deal.

- *noun* unsatisfactory substitute or imitation; from Latin *simulare* 'simulate'
- see also **bottled Brexit, jot and tittle, lapidary, muff it, polish a turd, Precambrian**

Sinophobia

'It has become a cliché to say China is the next world super power. It is stark staring nonsense. China will not dominate the globe. Our Sinophobia is misplaced.'

Daily Telegraph, 3 September 2005.

- Latin *Sinae* 'China'; Greek *phobos* 'fear'
- see also **human panda, Panatheic frieze, vertiginously, wiff-waff**

Sisyphean

'They told Dean about the horrors of this Sisyphean task, how even if the gum came off the flag, it adhered so grimly to the scraper that it seemed nothing would shift it but a tactical nuclear weapon.'

Seventy-Two Virgins, 2004.

- In Greek mythology, King Sisyphus was forced to roll a boulder up a hill only for it to roll down again for eternity
- see also **Augean, sword of Damocles, Tantalus**

Sjambok

'We can change the law to allow the police to administer sjambok drubbings, or we adults can … recognise that it is up to us to give young people hope, boundaries and a moral framework.'

Daily Telegraph, 14 August 2011.

- *noun* heavy leather whip; used by South African police during apartheid
- see also **banana-booted demigod, chavs, feckless, Maenads, medieval on their ass**

Skegness

'I say stuff Skegness. I say bugger Bognor … My trunks and I are off to the sun.'

Daily Telegraph, 22 July 2008.

On preferring foreign holidays to ones in faded English seaside resorts Skegness in Lincolnshire and Bognor Regis in West Sussex.

- stuff, abbreviated form of 'get stuffed'; bugger, Old French *bougre* via Latin *bulgaris*. 'Bugger Bognor' gained currency after these were (probably inaccurately) said to be the dying words of King George V in 1928
- see also **bugger**

Skull-piling warlord

'What Churchill did at Mers-el-Kébir was indeed butchery, but it was necessary. It was the chilling and calculated act of a skull-piling warlord from the steppes of Central Asia.'
The Churchill Factor, 2014.

Comparing Churchill's sinking of the French fleet in 1940 to the ruthlessness of warriors like Genghis Khan.

- *noun* bloodthirsty military leader
- see also **epiphenomena, funky Gibbon, Gibbonian, megalopsychia, numen, rumbustious, syllogism, transmogrifying, wangled, Zeus and Polyhymnia**

Snaggle-toothed lefties

'Corduroy-jacketed, snaggle-toothed, lefty academics.'
Speaking in Tel Aviv, 11 November 2015.

Caricaturing British supporters of the Israel boycott.

- *adjective* snaggle-toothed, having crooked teeth, from English 'snaggle, snag'

Snooks

'I decided in that moment of adrenalin and dopamine:

snooks to all of them. What is popularity but a sham, a snare, a delusion?'

Friends, Voters, Countrymen, 2001.

On dealing with character attacks as an MP.

- *noun* a derisive gesture; 'cocking a snook'; a sign of derision made, usually by children, by putting the thumb on the nose and wiggling the fingers; dopamine, natural compound linked to adrenalin
- see also **best of all worlds, cursus honorum, Disraeli and Achilles, ker-splonked**

Snooty

'I don't see why people are so snooty about Channel 5. It has some respectable documentaries about the Second World War. It also devoted considerable airtime to investigations into lap dancing, and other related and vital subjects.'

Daily Telegraph, 14 March 2002.

Defence of British TV station Channel 5, seen by some as down-market.

- *adjective* contempt for others, usually of lower class; haughtily looking down one's nose; snout, slang for nose
- see also **supercilious sibilance**

Snore-athon

'It feels like an attempt to keep the great snore-athon story about my article running.'

Interview in *The Guardian*, 19 September 2017.

Dismissing claims that he planned to resign as Foreign
Secretary over Theresa May's Brexit policy.

- Borisism
- *noun* boring; sleep-inducing nonsense
- see also **bottled Brexit, jot and tittle, muff it, polish a turd, schmoozathon, simulacrum**

Soi-disant poet

*'It was part of Virgil's claim to greatness that he was not
only the soi-disant poet of Roman imperialism...'*
The Dream of Rome, 2006.

- *adjective* self-styled, so-called; from French *soi* 'self', *disant* 'said'; literally 'self-said'
- see also **Aegyptia coniunx, equo ne credite, Teucri, nec tali auxilio, nec defensoribus istis**

Solon

*'I congratulate him on joining the tradition of great law-
makers such as Hammurabi, Solon and Moses, who made
laws on this very subject.'*
House of Commons, 16 May 2003.

Debating Sunday trading laws.

- Solon (c. 630 BC–c. 560 BC), Greek statesman who fought the moral, political and economic decline of Athens; Hammurabi, King of Babylon (1810 BC–1750 BC), introduced the Code of Hammurabi, among the first codes of law to establish the idea of presumption of innocence
- see also **hebdomadal, fasti**

Soutien-gorges

'I have read the average British male is incapable of keeping his mind off sex for more than three minutes. If we want to save jobs in that disaster-hit country ... we should lift the tariffs on brassieres, or soutien-gorges, as they are known in Brussels. It is outrageous that this bra tax should be going to Gordon Brown.'

Daily Telegraph, 6 January 2005.

Calling for EU tariffs on Sri Lankan exports of bras to be scrapped to help them recover from the tsunami.

- Borisism
- see also **Boobtropolis, bra-fetishist, ceaseless carnal activity, mega-titted, phallocratic phallus, poule de luxe, satyriasis**

Spaffed

'£60 million ... was being spaffed up a wall on some investigation into historic child abuse.'

LBC Radio, 13 March 2019.

Criticising the amount spent on investigating non-recent child abuse allegations against public figures.

- *verb* slang; to ejaculate, to waste
- see also **engine of Onan, onanistic, wankerer**

Spatchcocked

'The Further Education and Training Bill was a rushed job, spatchcocked together at the last minute.'

House of Commons, 15 March 2007.

Attack on Labour education plans.

- *verb* to insert a clause where it is not appropriate; to split open a piece of poultry to prepare it for cooking; 'dispatch' and 'cock'
- see also **Spheroids**

Spheroids

'Spheroids dismissed the idea that Latin could inspire or motivate pupils. Head teachers often took him to see the benefits of dance, or technology, or sport, said this intergalactic ass ... It is ... a disaster that this man is still nominally in charge of education...'

Daily Telegraph, 15 March 2010.

Savaging Labour Education Secretary Ed Balls for not promoting Latin in schools.

- Borisism
- *noun* spheroid; from Latin *sphaerodes* 'ball'
- see also **asphodel and mallow, bunkum, balderdash, tommyrot and fiddlesticks, Latinate evasion, namby-pamby, scansion, trud**

Spifflicated

'In the evening we canvass Watlington with Roger Belson, the county council candidate. Roger is a tall, good-looking, highly intelligent man who was spifflicated in a car crash.'

Friends, Voters, Countrymen, 2001.

- *verb* badly hurt; from eighteenth-century English, 'badly wounded'; possibly from 'suffocate' and 'spill'; from early twentieth century, 'drunk'
- see also **hogwhimpering, Maenads**

Spillikin

'Take out one spillikin from the heap of factors, and you can never tell how the rest will fall.'

The Churchill Factor, 2014.

On how easily the Second World War could have taken a different course.

- *noun* game played with a heap of small plastic sticks, in which players try to remove one at a time without disturbing the others
- see also **epiphenomena, Zeus and Polyhymnia**

Splutterissimo

'He went on to deplore the general phobia of risk in today's namby-pamby society ... the use of cup holders and – splutterissimo – air-bags in the new American tanks.'

Seventy-Two Virgins, 2004.

- Borisism
- *noun* exaggerated splutter caused by indignation; from Middle English *sputen* 'to spout' or 'to vomit'; Italian suffix *issimo* added for effect
- see also **dur-brained, namby-pamby, scabophobic**

Stakhanovite

'Happy backlit pictures of girls in summer dresses receiving the news of their Stakhanovite performances at A-level and GCSE.'

Daily Telegraph, 24 August 2009.

Describing the newspaper coverage of hard-working students waiting for exam results.

- *noun* worker in the former Soviet Union who was exceptionally productive; Alexey Stakhanov was a role model for hard work in the Soviet Union after mining over 200 tonnes of coal in a single shift in 1935
- see also **spatchcocked, Spheroids, trud**

Star-struck booby

'A *star-struck booby ... some have implied the President co-erced Miss Lewinsky. The more footage we see of them together, the more obvious it is that she transpires at every pore with lust to be noticed ... hanging around outside the Oval Office in a low-cut dress ... one is inclined to sympathise with the President.'*

- *noun* stupid person easily impressed by fame; booby, Spanish, *bobo*, via Latin *balbus* 'stammering'; boob, slang for breasts
- see also **buxom as all get out, dirndl, divine gift of lewdness, mega-titted, pouty sadistic nurse**

Stilton-eating surrender monkeys

'*The Lords was full of Stilton-eating surrender monkeys.*'
The Churchill Factor, 2014.

Describing peers who wanted to appease Hitler.

- *noun* borrowed from pejorative term for French people; 'cheese-eating surrender monkeys' first appeared in US cartoon *The Simpsons*. Apocryphally used by George W. Bush to attack the French government for not supporting him over the 2003 Iraq War.
- see also **buzzard squint, crack-brained neocons, dada-ist, Kylie's rear, orally extemporising, quislings, Schindler, weevilled**

Stonkingly rich

'I neither resent nor approve of such zillionaires; quite the reverse. I just wonder, a bit, what it is like to be so stonkingly rich.'

Daily Telegraph, 17 November 2013.

- *adverb* wealthy to an impressive extent; stonk, First World War British military slang for heavy bombardment
- see also **buttock exposure**

Stooge

'The terrible art of the candidate is to coddle the self-deception of the stooge.'

Chapter in *The Oxford Myth*, edited by Boris's sister Rachel Johnson, 1988.

On how to campaign successfully for the presidency of the Oxford Union. Fellow Oxford graduate Michael Gove says he played the role of 'stooge – a votary of the Boris cult' to help Johnson win in 1985.

- *noun* derogatory term for someone who gets someone else to do their dirty work; origin unknown, 1920s American
- see also **Aryan bull pig, Buller, coddle**

Striated

'He panted as he tried to lug the inert mass of the President across the old striated shale.'

Seventy-Two Virgins, 2004.

- *adjective* striped or streaked; from Latin *striatus* 'to groove' or 'to flute'

Strigil

'Perhaps even using [an ID card] as a kind of strigil, as they did back in ancient Athens, to scrape off the mixture of sweat and olive oil when you have been for an exhausting run.'

Daily Telegraph, 24 November 2004.

Suggesting alternative uses for ID cards following Labour's announcement of plans to introduce them.

- *noun* scraper; from Latin *strigil*, Roman curved metal bathing tool used to scrape oil and dirt from the skin
- see also **breaking and entering, impis**

Stuffed

'Get stuffed.'

City Hall, London, 2014.

During an angry exchange as London Mayor with Labour opponent Andrew Dismore, who accused him of lying about cuts in the capital's fire service.

- slang, 'go screw yourself'
- see also **condom stuffed with walnuts, puffed-up popinjay**

Stumblebum

'Would I be an orator to match Hezza? Were the people of Henley wise to replace such a snappy dresser with a man in stumblebum suits?'

Friends, Voters, Countrymen, 2001.

On following in the footsteps of Michael Heseltine as MP for Henley.

- *noun* clumsy, inept; amalgamation of 'stumble' and 'bum'

- see also **chunderous, defenestrating, Simba**

Stung in the bum

'My foot pressed down and, yeeeow! the blue streak of tin-plated testosterone surged ahead like some stallion stung in the bum by a bee.'

Life in the Fast Lane, 2007.

On driving a Nissan Skyline.

- see also **flaccidity, fully extended bonk, gynaecomorphised, Italian stallion, non-turgor factor, phallocratic phallus, pingoaded stallion, tinplate testosterone**

Stupefying ignorance

'Donald Trump is betraying a quite stupefying ignorance that makes him frankly unfit to hold the office of President.'

The Independent, 9 December 2015.

Responding to Trump's claim that there were lawless 'no-go areas' in London because of large Muslim populations.

- stupefy, Latin *stupefacere*, meaning 'make stupid or senseless'
- see also **crack-brained neocons, egotistical glory-mania, monochrome Manichean, progenitor, puffed-up popinjay, whinge-o-rama**

Superannuated taramasalata

'Saddam Hussein boasted no WMD more fearful than a tub of superannuated taramasalata.'

Daily Telegraph, 29 April 2004.

Ridiculing Tony Blair's claims about the threat from Iraq's outdated chemical weapon stockpile.

- superannuated, out of date, obsolete; from Latin *super* 'beyond', 'over', and *annus* 'year'; taramasalata, a Greek meze made from fish roe
- see also **casus belli, cobblers, greased piglet, schlockiest bonkbuster**

Supercilious sibilance

'It was the revenge of the bar-bar-barbarians upon the entire supercilious sibilance of the Latin language.'
The Dream of Rome, 2006.
Describing a thuggish German warrior taking pleasure in cutting out the tongue of a Roman army officer.

- Borisism
- *noun* Latin *superciliosus* 'haughty', via *supercilium* 'eyebrow'; sibilance, hissing sounds produced by stressing consonants through lips and tongue; from Latin *sibilare* 'hiss'
- see also **Cannae, pudding basin, seal-skin jockstrap, snooty**

Super-colossal pickled onion

'It's like the tip of a cocktail stick emerging through the skin of a super-colossal pickled onion.'
The opening of London skyscraper the Shard, 1 February 2013.

Supererogatory

'We are giving [those guarantees] unilaterally, in a super-erogatory way.'
House of Commons, 25 July 2019.

Response when challenged over whether EU citizens would have a right to stay in the UK after Brexit.

- *adjective* doing more than is asked for; from Latin *super* 'above', *erogo* 'pay out'
- see also **Bre-entry**

Suppressio veri and suggestio falsi

'*It was heart rending to someone who has acquired the scaly carapace necessary for dealing with the politico-journalistic complex. … it is so habituated to spin, half-truth, suppressio veri and suggestio falsi they are genuinely unable to tell when they are guilty of these practices themselves.*'
Daily Telegraph, 4 September 2003.

Contrasting the courage and honesty of Janice Kelly at the 2003 Hutton Inquiry into the death of her husband, MoD weapons expert Dr David Kelly, to the cynical distortions of politicians and the press.

- *idiom* suppressing the truth is equivalent to suggesting a falsehood; Latin *suppressio* 'suppress'; *veri* 'truth'; *falsi* 'false'; carapace, hard shell, Portuguese *carapace* 'shell'
- see also **glow-worm transience**, **nel mezzo del cammin di nostra vita**, **pshaw**, **sandpapered**, **swankpot journalists**

Surefire destitution

'*If having a baby out of wedlock meant surefire destitution on a Victorian scale, young girls might … think twice about having a baby.*'
The Spectator, 1995.

Calling for tough action to curb teenage pregnancies.

- Borisism
- guaranteed poverty or hardship
- see also **chavs, feckless, Maenads**

Swankpot journalists

'The world ought not to be run by swankpot journalists, showing off and kicking politicians around, when they haven't tried to do any better themselves...'

Friends, Voters, Countrymen, 2001.

On why he entered politics.

- Borisism
- origin unknown; 'to swank' can mean to strut, to behave ostentatiously
- see also **boondoggle, epiphytes, glow-worm transience, pshaw, Roman swanking, suppressio veri and suggestio falsi, vaginal endearment**

Switcheroo

'Anthropologists will look back with awe at the change that took place in our national mood – the sudden switcheroo from the gloom of the previous weeks.'

Conservative Party conference, 9 October 2012.

On the success of the London Olympics.

- Borisism
- *noun* sudden change, reversal; first recorded in 1933; from 'switch'
- see also **eudaimonia, gobsmacked, Ready Brek glow, vaginal endearment, wet otters, zoink**

Sword of Damocles

'The public can be forgiven for genuinely starting to wonder whether the nuclear sword of Damocles is once again held over the head of a trembling human race.'

Speech at Chatham House think tank, 23 October 2017.

On the threat from North Korea.

- From Greek mythology; Damocles was a courtier forced to sit beneath a sword suspended by a single hair to symbolise the instability of a king's fortunes
- see also **dada-ist, Mexican stand-off, Nobel Peace Prize, Sisyphean, ululations**

Syllogism

'I have always thought Churchill had a secret syllogism in his head: Britain is the greatest empire on Earth. Churchill is the greatest man in the British Empire. Therefore Churchill is the greatest man on Earth.'

The Churchill Factor, 2014.

- *noun* arriving at a conclusion by examining two other premises or ideas; from Old French *silogisme*, scholastic argument based on a formula or proof, and Greek *sullogismos*, *sun-* 'with', *logos* 'reasoning'
- see also **anaphora, chiasmus, epiphenomena, megalopsychia, numen, world king, Zeus and Polyhymnia**

Syncretic

'[Manchester is] a society that does not judge you for where you come from or your background or how you live

your life provided you do no harm to others. That is the syncretic genius of our country.'

Conservative Party conference, Manchester, 3 October 2017.

- *noun* combining different beliefs; from Latin *syncretismus* via Greek *synkretismos*

- see also **acculturated, Kulturkampf, natural as sewage, piss against the wall, re-Britannification, verkrampte, xenophobe**

T

Taliban chappies
'There will be plenty of British Conservatives who think these Taliban chappies run a tight ship, women's lib is not an unalloyed blessing, look at all these poofters these days, and so on.'
Daily Telegraph, 27 September 2001.
Lampooning the opposition of traditional Conservative supporters to gay rights and women's liberation.

- *noun* Taliban, Islamic fundamentalist movement in Afghanistan; poofters, homophobic slur, corruption of puff
- see also **pathetic Islamofascists**, **scum**, **tank-topped bumboys**, **towelhead nutters**

Tank-topped bumboys
'Weep, O ye shirt-makers of Jermyn Street, ye Cool Britannia tailors ... The tank-topped bumboys blub into their Pils ... For Mandy is dead.'
Daily Telegraph, 24 December 1998.

On Peter Mandelson's resignation from the Labour Cabinet, which came shortly after he was outed as gay.

- Borisism
- *noun* offensive description of trendy young gay men
- see also **buttock exposure, camp Plantagenets, consecrated, sexist fronde, Taliban chappies, up the Arcelor**

Tantalus

'Like Tantalus in Hades, we can see the opportunities in front of us – the luscious grapes, the refreshing stream – and yet every time we reach out to grasp them we find they are whisked away.'

Daily Telegraph, 5 November 2019.

On Parliament's Brexit deadlock.

- From Greek mythology; for attempting to serve up his own son, Pelops, at a feast for the gods, Tantalus was sentenced to forever go thirsty and hungry in Hades, despite being stood in a pool of water almost within reach of a fruit tree
- see also **autarkic, bottled Brexit, Bre-entry, Brexchosis, muff it, Scylla and Charybdis, Sisyphean, sword of Damocles, whey**

Tattooed bottoms

'There is no reason we should pay for people to have tattoos removed from their bottoms. The middle classes should be required to stump up for non-essential services … If NHS services continue to be free in this way, they will continue to be abused. If people have to pay, they will value them more.'

The Spectator, 23 September 1995.

On paying for the NHS.

- see also **bottom pat, buttock exposure, dolts and serfs, hubble-bubble pipe, Kylie's rear, Maenads, not on the table, parable of the toast**

Taxidermy

'He is a sort of lapdog of David Cameron who's been converted by taxidermy into a kind of protective shield, like the Emperor Valerian, who was skinned and hung on the wall.'

ITV interview, 13 December 2013.

Poking fun at Liberal Democrat Nick Clegg, then Deputy Prime Minister in David Cameron's coalition government.

- *noun* art of stuffing the skins of animals, from Greek *taxis* 'skin', *derma* 'skin'; Valerian, Roman Emperor from 253 AD to 260 AD, was captured by a Persian king who had his skin stuffed with straw and preserved as a trophy
- see also **Cleggster, condom stuffed with walnuts, Hyrcanian tiger, yellow albatross**

Tenax propositi

'In theory, it is a measure of a statesman's fitness for power whether he is tenax propositi, whether he adheres to principle.'

The Spectator, 29 April 1995.

Accusing Tony Blair of lacking principle.

- *noun* firm of purpose; from Latin *tenax* 'hold fast', *propositum* 'proposal'

- see also **Archaiser, guff, semolina blob, whiffled, witchetty grub**

Testadicazzo

'Have you ever driven very fast on a motorway? I have. Not long ago, I found myself at the wheel of a Ferrari Testadicazzo, or some such name, capable of 220mph. Who needs a car that fast, you ask … to bust out of the comfortable old corset of the 70mph restriction? It's you. It's me. It's everyone.'
Daily Telegraph, 12 July 2001.

Calling to raise the UK speed limit. There is no Ferrari Testadicazzo; it is Italian slang for 'dickhead'.

- Borisism
- *testa*, Italian, 'head'; *cazzo*, Italian, 'cock', 'dick'
- see also **aire fe Mabda'ak, braggadocio, donger, endocrine orchestra, Italian stallion, motability rickshaws, phallocratic phallus**

Thrumming

'My realistic chances of becoming Prime Minister are only slightly better than my chances of being decapitated by a Frisbee, blinded by a champagne cork, locked in a disused fridge … I'm forty-seven now. I hear the thrumming roar of young men in a hurry. And young women, obviously.'
Hay Literary Festival, 3 June 2012.

- *verb* continuous rhythmic humming sound; from Old English *thrum*, ligament of the tongue
- see also **bumbling skill, Cincinnatus, cursus honorum, Disraeli and Achilles, imbecilio, Latinate evasion, reincarnated as an olive, wise guy**

Tiggerish

'*Some people find him too Tiggerish and bumptious. I have been in a state of glorious detachment on the Sarkozy issue – until I read that he was once again under attack from French intellectuals ... these heirs of Sartre and Saussure [say that] the very act of le jogging ... is a cultural humiliation.*'

Daily Telegraph, 5 July 2007.

Defending fellow jogger Nicolas Sarkozy after the French President was criticised for it in France.

- *adjective* lively, energetic, cheerful; Tigger, fictional tiger in A. A. Milne's *Winnie the Pooh* children's books
- see also **rumbustious, runty kid**

Tiglath-Pileser

'*Saddam banned the packs as somehow un-Baathist, though they have been a part of Mesopotamian life since ... Tiglath-Pileser set off in his chariot in search of a lion.*'

Seventy-Two Virgins, 2004.

A character in the novel's criticism of Iraqi dictator Saddam Hussein for banning hunting with dogs.

- Tiglath-Pileser I (1114 BC–1076 BC), King of Assyria (which includes part of modern Iraq) who boasted of killing more than 900 lions
- see also **Brueghelian, cauls, gift of death, gralloched, semolina blob, sexual yipping, tweed-wearing atavism**

Time of day

'Was there no one in this goddamn country who wanted to take her firmly in his arms and give a girl the time of day?'
Seventy-Two Virgins, 2004.

Female American character complaining about the lack of sexual vigour in British men.

- *noun* show interest in someone; slang for sexual intercourse. First appears in J. D. Salinger's 1951 novel *The Catcher in the Rye*; Holden Caulfield says, 'Hey man, I told her "the time" last night … if you know what I mean.'
- see also **Dorking Rugby Club's second XV, flaccidity, imperial good-time girls, non-turgor factor, phallocratic phallus, satyriasis**

Timorousness

'The government have yet to decide whether, owing to the Prime Minister's timorousness on the subject, they have the guts to call a referendum.'
2003.

On Tony Blair's refusal to call a referendum on joining the euro.

- *noun* nervousness, timidity; from Latin *timere* 'to fear'
- see also **guff, infinite sagacity, protozoan, whiffle**

Tinplate testosterone

'A man endlessly fascinated by the various advantages and disappointments of his own gonads. He had Bentleys bulging with tinplate testosterone … he echoed the hedonistic

juvenile vroom vroom obsessions of anyone who reads a lads' mag.'

Daily Telegraph, 9 September 1999.

On the death of Tory MP and diarist Alan Clark.

• see also **endocrine orchestra, gynaecomorphised, Latinate evasion, stung in the bum, upper epidermis of the gonad**

Tits in a wringer

'We will be fighting this all the way. I am very sorry that Alastair Campbell has taken this decision but I can see that he's got his tits in a wringer.'

The Spectator, April 2002.

After Tony Blair's spin doctor Alastair Campbell complained about a story by Peter Oborne in the magazine, which stated that Blair had 'muscled in' on the Queen Mother's funeral. The complaint was dropped.

• *idiom* crude slang, to get upset; wringers, old-style washing machines with two cylinders between which laundry was wrung out; to catch any part of the body in it would be painful (especially a 'tit', breast). Origin, *Derek and Clive*, 1970s BBC TV show: 'I haven't laughed so much since Grandma caught her left tit in the mangle.'

• see also **bizzaz immak ala amood, guff, mordant paradox, pshaw**

Toad beneath the harrow

'Brexit will be crushed like the toad beneath the harrow.'

Text message to David Cameron, 21 February 2016.

Sent moments before he announced he would lead the Brexit campaign – while claiming it would fail.

- *idiom* stress, suffering; a harrow is a heavy frame with spikes dragged across a field by horses or a tractor to cultivate the soil. A toad beneath it would have no chance of survival. From Rudyard Kipling's poem about fictitious politician Pagett MP, 'a fluent liar':

    The toad beneath the harrow knows
    Exactly where each tooth-point goes.

- see also **demotic, Eurydice, girly swot, inverted pyramid of piffle, Latinate evasion, Scarface, schmoozathon, torrents of obfuscation**

Torrents of obfuscation

'This week was the moment when the world decided to say enough to the wearying barrage of Russian lies, the torrent of obfuscation and intercontinental ballistic whoppers.'

Speaking at Mansion House, London, 28 March 2018.

Applauding international support for the UK over the poisoning of Russian double agent Sergei Skripal and daughter Yulia in Salisbury.

- *noun* making something obscure, unclear, or unintelligible; torrent, strong river flow; obfuscation, from Latin *obfuscationem* 'to darken'
- see also **Dobby, media ectoplasm**

Tory tosser

'If someone said, "You Tory tosser," I would take it as a badge of honour.'

- *noun* coarse slang; unpleasant or contemptible individual; someone who tosses
- see also **blubbering ninny, donger, engine of Onan, onanistic, selfish tosser, spaffed, wankerer**

Tottometer

'It is what is called the Tottometer, the geigercounter that detects good-looking women. In 1997, I reported, these were to be found in numbers at the Labour conference. Now ... the Tories are fighting back.'

The Spectator, 10 February 2001.

Using the number of attractive women at party conferences as a way of measuring its popularity.

- Borisism
- 'posh totty', attractive upper-class females; tot, English, 'small child'
- see also **Araminta, bag of ferrets, gynaecomorphised, hunchoswingometer, imperial good-time girls, phallocratic phallus**

Toutatis

'Aiee, they cry. You have been warned! You have been warmed. The raingods are angry with mankind: Thor, Toutatis, Iuppiter Pluvius, drumming their fingers on our roofs, impatient at our frivolity ... Forget the green doomsters.'

Daily Telegraph, 2 November 2000.

Mocking climate change protestors.

- Toutatis, a Celtic God in ancient Britain and Gaul; catchphrase 'By Toutatis!' appears in the French *Asterix* comics. Thor, god of thunder in Germanic mythology; Jupiter (alt. spelling Juppiter); Pluvius, Roman god of rainstorms
- see also **Brahmaputra, Caracas, chitterlings and chine, hempen, Heisenberg, vertiginously**

Towelhead nutters

'Americans voted in huge numbers to vindicate their right to bang up the towelhead nutters.'

Seventy-Two Virgins, 2004.

- *noun* slang for insane person of certain ethnic origins; racial slur, derived from the turbans or other headwear worn by Muslims, Arabs, Sikhs and others
- see also **crack-brained neocons, pathetic Islamofascists, stupefying ignorance, Taliban chappies, Wahhabi lust**

Toxoplasmosis

'There was steak tartare, so eloquent of toxoplasmosis that in her country it would have been banned by the Food and Drug Administration.'

Seventy-Two Virgins, 2004.

- *noun* parasitic disease; from Greek *toxo* 'poison', *plasma* 'mould, shape'
- see also **chitterlings and chine, dikbil, dur-brained, encephalopathic**

Trabeate and arcuate

'Ephesus was a Roman city somehow growing originally out of Greek civilisation … it's trabeate and arcuate at once.'

The Dream of Rome, 2006.

- *adjective(s)* contrasting Classical architectural styles; trabeate architecture, roofs and doors are supported by a horizontal beam across vertical columns; arcuate relies on arches
- see also **Panatheic frieze**

Transmogrifying

'Churchill was transmogrifying himself into the spirit of the nation, the very emblem of defiance.'

The Churchill Factor, 2014.

- *verb* to transmogrify; to transform, often in a comic manner; from Latin *trans* 'across'; 'transmogrify' first appears in a play by seventeenth-century dramatist Aphra Behn: 'I wou'd Love would transmogriphy me to a maid now'
- see also **epiphenomena, funky Gibbon, megalopsychia, syllogism, wangled, Zeus and Polyhymnia**

Trud

'[The Labour Party] exalt WORK with all the mania of 1930s Soviet agitprop extolling the virtues of trud, with meaty-forearmed hammer-wielding women rolling up their sleeves and preparing to join the men at the lathe.'

The Spectator, 23 May 2007.

Attacking the 'new Puritanism' of Labour Chancellor Gordon Brown.

- *noun* hard work; graft; from Russian, meaning 'labour'
- see also **asphodel and mallow, filching, gelatinous, Gordonomics, Spheroids, Stakhanovite**

Tsavo

'Sometimes I worry that the British electorate has acquired a bad habit, like the man-eaters of Tsavo.'

Friends, Voters, Countrymen, 2001.

- Man-eating lions in Africa's Tsavo region killed men working on the Kenya–Uganda Railway in 1898
- see also **charismatic megafauna, Hyrcanian tiger, impis, prelapsarian**

Turnip ghost

'He held up ... a turnip-ghost, called "the forces of Conservatism", and he invited his audience to heap their scorn on today's Tory Party ... There was no evil which could not be laid at the door of these "forces of conservatism." It was a hideous and cynical smear.'

The Spectator, 2 October 1999.

Attacking Tony Blair.

- *noun* bogeyman; turnip ghost, apparition with a head in the shape of a turnip; term of abuse in bygone days
- see also **drag artistry, Goebbels-esque fallaciousness, guff**

Tweed-wearing atavism

'The quarrel over hunting enables Labour ministers to caricature their opponents as tweed-wearing Waugh-reading defenders of atavism.'

Daily Telegraph, 18 January 2001.

On Labour's opposition to hunting.

- atavism, tendency to revert to something ancient, from Latin *atavus* 'forefather'; Evelyn Waugh was the author of *Brideshead Revisited*, a 1945 novel about the 1920s English ruling class
- see also **Brueghelian, cauls, charismatic megafauna, gift of death, gralloched, semolina blob, sexual yipping, Tiglath-Pileser**

Twitter-borne transphobes

'Are you really telling me that it is a sensible ordering of priorities to round up Twitter-borne transphobes and chuck them in the clink?'

Daily Telegraph, 10 February 2019.

Criticising police arrests of those who abuse transgender people on social media instead of those committing violent crime.

- Borisism
- transphobe, Latin *trans* 'across'; Greek *phobos* 'fear, phobia'
- see also **blubbering ninny, engine of Onan, jabberama, pullulate**

Two-seater chickwagon

'A long nozzled, two seater chickwagon … designed for joy and fun … everything except the mental torture of having the chick … squirming on your lap in a seriously frictional manner. I groan as the sap rises. Has she noticed … her chest is in my face and oooooof.'

Life in the Fast Lane, 2007.

On riding in the passenger seat of an MG sports car with a girl on his lap.

- Borisism
- see also **endocrine orchestra, fully extended bonk, gynaecomorphised, Italian stallion, one-eyed trouser snake**

u

Ululations

'He could move the women of Greenham Common and the Tory conference to alternate ululations of hatred and sexual rapture.'

Friends, Voters, Countrymen, 2001.

Describing Michael Heseltine, loathed by anti-nuclear protestors at the RAF Greenham Common US missile base; loved by female Conservative supporters.

- *noun* long, wavering, high-pitched vocal sound resembling a howl; from Latin *ululo* 'screech'
- see also **chunderous, entasis, matricide, pharaonic Hezzapolis, Simba**

Umbilicus

'My hon. Friend has hit upon the notion of a metaphorical fixed link: a great, swollen, throbbing umbilicus of trade ... with each side mutually nourishing the other.'

House of Commons, 20 February 2019.

On the importance of UK trade with the EU.

* *noun* umbilical cord channels blood to foetus during pregnancy; from Latin, navel
* see also **autarkic, boosterism, Bre-entry, gloomadon-poppers, penumbra, whey**

Unclove

'Buttock after buttock unclove itself from the little gilt chairs.'
Seventy-Two Virgins, 2004.

Describing relieved VIPs when help arrives during a terror attack in Westminster Hall.

* *verb* to uncleave; detach; from Latin *clavus* 'nail'
* see also **buttock exposure, buttock-headed, gibbering rictus, up the Arcelor**

Up the Arcelor

'It will be the perfect ceremony, you can take your partner up the Arcelor.'
2013.

Joking that gay couples could marry at the ArcelorMittal Orbit, a 115-metre tower at London's Olympic stadium. A Labour critic called it a 'phallic symbol of Johnson's ego.'

* Borisism
* see also **camp Plantagenets, sexist fronde, Taliban chappies, tank-topped bumboys**

Upper epidermis of the gonad

'Ah, yes. I'm on the upper epidermis of the gonad. Some-where near the seminal vesicle, I expect.'

6 June 2008.

On his mayoral office in London's City Hall, nicknamed 'the glass testicle' owing to its bulbous shape.

- Borisism
- *noun(s)* gonad, slang for testicle; epidermis, layer of skin; seminal vesicles, glands that produce semen
- see also **bag of ferrets, cobblers, get stuffed, phallocratic phallus, spaffed, tinplate testosterone**

V

Vaginal endearment

'*A great and famous editor of a much-loved family news-paper is said to have approached his backbench on the eve of the opening ceremony and addressed them with his usual vaginal endearment. "Now look here, you c***s, this is going to be one disaster after another. That's how I expect you to cover it."*'

The Spirit of London, 2012.

On alleged comments by an unnamed editor on the eve of the Olympics.

* Borisism
* See also **blubbering ninny, gobsmacked, gynaecomorphised, queynte, Ready Brek glow, swankpot journalists**

Vanilla nothingness

'*The vanilla nothingness of Blairism*'

Friends, Voters, Countrymen, 2001.

* *adjective* vanilla, off-white colour, slang for bland, boring
* see also **Archaiser, guff, infinite sagacity, semolina blob, whiffled**

Verkrampte

'He was right, in his verkrampte way ... Britain might or might not be becoming a mongrel nation ... But it was a lie to suggest that the British had always been in just such a state of rapid ethnic diversification.'

Friends, Voters, Countrymen, 2001.

On a Tory MP who was criticised for saying the UK had become a 'mongrel nation'.

- *adjective* Afrikaans, 'conservative', bigoted or reactionary
- see also **acculturated, burqa, Little Britons, re-Britannification, xenophobe**

Vertiginously

'May I respectfully suggest to the Extinction Rebellion crew that next Earth Day they look at China, where CO₂ output has not been falling, but rising vertiginously. Take their pink boat to China and lecture them.'

Daily Telegraph, 21 April 2019.

Suggesting climate change campaigners who brought London to a halt with a pink boat on a truck should focus their protests on China.

- *adverb* rising to a high level; dizziness caused by extreme height; Latin *vertigo* 'whirling about'
- see also **Brahmaputra, Caracas, chitterlings and chine, hempen, Heisenberg, Sinophobia**

Vinegarish

'I switched from a position of moderate idealism to one of fairly vinegarish scepticism.'

Friends, Voters, Countrymen, 2001.

On changing his view on the EU in his years as a Brussels correspondent.

- *adjective* having a sour disposition; ill-tempered
- see also **bibble-babble, fungible, give a monkey's, homo foederalis, Procrustean squeezing**

Vole-trousered

'He has an innocent and vole-trousered air but his domestic policies would rack up unfair debts for our children and grandchildren and his foreign policies would imperil not just this country but our friends and neighbours as well.'

Conservative Party conference, 3 October 2017.

Describing Jeremy Corbyn.

- *noun* reference to brand of weatherproof trousers
- see also **Caracas, Heisenberg, hempen, ignoratio elenchi, lachrymose, mutton-headed old mugwump, pushmi-pullyu**

W

Wahhabi lust

'He stared with that perverted Wahhabi mixture of lust, terror and disgust at this portrait of sexually emancipated Western woman.'

Seventy-Two Virgins, 2004.

An Islamic fundamentalist terrorist's complicated feelings towards an American woman.

- *noun* Wahhabi is the conservative branch within Islam's Sunni branch
- see also **ceaseless carnal activity, divine gift of lewdness, pathetic Islamofascists, poule de luxe, raisins, scum, sexually liberated, sharmoota**

Wangled

'If you want to understand how he won the war, look at the way he wangled and wheedled his way to Washington.'

The Churchill Factor, 2014.

- *verb* obtain something by persuasion or clever manipulation
- see also **epiphenomena, funky Gibbon, Gibbonian, megalopsychia,**

numen, orotund, rumbustious, skull-piling warlord, syllogism, transmogrifying, Zeus and Polyhymnia

Wankerer

'There was a young fellow from Ankara,
Who was a terrific wankerer…'
The Spectator, 18 May 2016.

From Johnson's winning entry for a 'President Erdoğan Offensive Poetry' competition.

- Borisism
- see also **donger, engine of Onan, epic poem, Johnson-oglus, onanistic, scansion, selfish tosser, spaffed, Tory tosser**

Watermelon smiles

'Blair is off to the Congo. No doubt the AK47s will fall silent, and the pangas will stop their hacking of human flesh, and the tribal warriors will all break out in watermelon smiles to see the big white chief touch down in his big white British taxpayer-funded bird.'
Daily Telegraph, 10 January 2002.

On Tony Blair's visit to Africa.

- *noun* nineteenth-century American racial slur. Watermelons were a favourite fruit of slaves who grew them to celebrate being freed. Southern white supremacists responded by making 'watermelon smiles' a racist symbol of the freed slaves' perceived laziness; panga, machete
- see also **Archaiser, flag-waving piccaninnies, Hottentot**

Weevilled

'The British ruling class was riddled – at least conspicuously weevilled – with appeasers and pro-Nazis.'

The Churchill Factor, 2014.

- *noun* weevil, small beetle that bores into plants and crops and destroys them; from Old English *wifel* 'small beetle'
- see also **pusillanimously, quislings, Stilton-eating surrender monkeys**

Wenching

'It was expressly permitted … for a Roman man to have any kind of liaison with anyone who was not a married Roman woman – that meant all sorts of wenching with slave girls and prostitutes.'

The Dream of Rome, 2006.

- from Old English *wenche* 'girl' or 'young maid'
- see also **bit of black, ceaseless carnal activity, fantastic goer, imperial good-time girls, poule de luxe, sharmoota**

Wet otters

'There are semi-naked women playing beach volleyball … glistening like wet otters.'

Daily Telegraph, 30 July 2012.

On women's volleyball in the London Olympics.

- *noun* otter, carnivorous, semi-aquatic mammal
- see also **little otter, Pindaric, switcheroo, zoink**

Whackos

'It may be that there are some readers so suspicious of politicians that they cannot believe anyone would want the job, except power-maniacs, freaks and whackos.'

Friends, Voters, Countrymen, 2001.

- *noun* a crazy person; alteration of whacky, a fool. Possibly derived from being 'whacked' on the head too many times
- see also **cursus honorum, Disraeli and Achilles, mordant paradox, phallocratic phallus, stupefying ignorance, thrumming, world king**

Whey

'I prophesy a successful Brexit, the planes will fly, there'll be clean drinking water and there will be whey for the Mars Bars. Because where there's a will there's a whey.'

Conservative leadership hustings, 27 June 2019.

- Borisism
- *noun* liquid remaining after milk is curdled and strained; it was reported the UK could run out of Mars Bars due to Brexit delays with imported whey
- see also **autarkic, boosterism, Bre-entry, Bremain, fuck business, muff it, murrain, pro having cake and pro eating it, umbilicus**

Whiffled

'He whiffled.'

1996.

On Tony Blair's oratory.

- Borisism

- *verb* to whiffle; modern usage, to change your opinion easily, making it hard for others to pin you down. Old English origin, 'wifel', via German, 'battle-axe'
- see also **buttock exposure, guff, lurve, turnip ghost, vanilla nothingness**

Whinge-o-rama

'I say to my beloved European friends and colleagues that it's time that we snapped out of the general doom and gloom about the result and collective whinge-o-rama going on in some places.'

11 November 2016.

Speaking after Donald Trump's election as President in 2016 was denounced by leading European politicians.

- Borisism
- *noun* whinge, excessive amount of complaining; from German *winseln* 'whine'
- see also **crack-brained neocons, Nobel Peace Prize, progenitor, puffed-up popinjay, stupefying ignorance**

Wiff-waff

'Ping-pong was invented on the dining tables of England in the nineteenth century, and it was called wiff-waff! ... Ping pong is coming home.'

Ceremonial handover of Olympic flag to UK in China in after 2008 Beijing Games, 25 August 2008.

Johnson claimed 'wiff-waff' was the name given to table tennis in Victorian England.

- see also **gobsmacked, human panda, Sinophobia, vaginal endearments**

Wise guy

'A wise guy playing the fool to win.'

Sunday Times, 16 July 2000.

On himself.

- *noun* someone who makes cheeky or sarcastic remarks to show off their intelligence
- see also **bufferdom, buffoonery, bumbling skill, imbecilio, Latinate evasion, thrumming**

Witchetty grub

'No, no, he kept saying yesterday, as he wriggled before Michael Howard like a kebabbed witchetty grub.'

Daily Telegraph, 8 January 2004.

Tony Blair denying to Conservative leader Michael Howard that he authorised the naming of MoD weapons expert Dr David Kelly, who subsequently committed suicide.

- *noun* Australian term for large, white, wood-eating larvae of several moths
- see also **pretzel-words, schlockiest bonkbuster, superannuated taramasalata, vanilla nothingness, whiffled**

Witenagemot

'The ealdormen and members of the witenagemot of Henley were there with their massy chains of office.'

Friends, Voters, Countrymen, 2001.

On meeting local dignitaries in Henley.

- *noun* Anglo-Saxon national council or parliament; from Old English *wita* 'man of knowledge'; *gemot* 'assembly'

Wog

'Here were the higgledy-piggledy headstones of the Arbuthnot family, sticking out of the earth like carious teeth. "Fuck off, wogs," wrote Dean on the Arbuthnots.'

Seventy-Two Virgins, 2004.

- *noun* racist term for a non-white person; thought to be abbreviation of 'golliwog', black-faced minstrel doll in a 1895 children's book
- see also **half-caste, Hottentot, puffing coolies, watermelon smiles**

World king

'I want to be world king.'

The Times, 2018.

Responding to sister Rachel when asked as a young child what he wanted to be when he grew up.

- Borisism
- see also **Cincinnatus, cursus honorum, Disraeli and Achilles, egotistical glory-mania, phallocratic phallus, runty kid, syllogism**

X

Xenophobe

'I'm not a xenophobe or someone who deprecates other countries and cultures. I'm called Boris, apart from anything else.'

19 January 2019.

Responding to claims that he did not like foreigners.

- *noun* person who is prejudiced against people from other countries; from Greek *xeno* 'foreign' or 'strange'; *phobe* 'fear'
- see also **acculturated, Aryan bull pig, burqa, Johnson-oglus, Kulturkampf, piss against the wall, Sinophobia, syncretic**

X

Y

Yellow albatross
'Insofar as he fulfils any function at all, it is to stop sensible policy being promulgated by this government. The sooner we are shot of the great yellow albatross the better.'
17 December 2013.
Accusing Lib Dem leader Nick Clegg of using his position as Deputy Prime Minister in David Cameron's government to veto Conservative policies.

- Borisism
- *idiom* a Lib Dem burden, curse; in Samuel Taylor Coleridge's poem 'The Rime of the Ancient Mariner', a sailor who shoots an albatross is forced to wear it round his neck as a punishment; yellow is the colour of the Liberal Democrats' logo; also synonymous with cowardice
- see also **Cleggster, inanation, taxidermy**

Yerked
'It would on the whole be better not to end up like the poor traffic warden, yerked beneath the breastbone, with the

bright bronchial blood still bubbling about the nose and mouth.'

Seventy-Two Virgins, 2004.

- *verb* to yerk; struck sharply; from late Middle English, imitative of sudden movement
- see also **gralloched**

Yokemates

'*Mr Blobby and Beethoven are yokemates of broadcasting destiny.*'

Daily Telegraph, 16 August 2008.

Defending the BBC licence fee by arguing it had to provide light and serious programmes, from Mr Blobby, a round pink character with yellow spots in a popular TV show, to classical composers.

- *noun* a person or thing closely linked or associated with another in some way; a yoke, bar or frame of wood which links oxen by the neck

Z

Zeus and Polyhymnia

'We think of him as somehow supernaturally gifted, as if he had sprung from a union of Zeus and Polyhymnia the very Muse of Rhetoric. I am afraid we are only partly right.'

The Churchill Factor, 2014.

Paying tribute to the full range of Churchill's talents.

- Zeus, supreme ruler of the gods; Polyhymnia, the muse of poetry, eloquence and pantomime
- see also **anaphora, chiasmus, dash of Dawson, epiphenomena, funky Gibbon, megalopsychia, numen, syllogism**

Ziggurats

'It would be wonderful if people were attracted by the cradle of civilisation, the ziggurats at Ur and the hanging gardens of Babylon, such as are left after the depredations of Saddam.'

26 May 2004.

Calling for the return of tourism to Iraq in a Westminster Hall debate.

- *noun* temple built in twenty-first century BC situated in modern-day Iraq
- see also **superannuated taramasalata**

Zingers

'Short, Anglo-Saxon zingers.'
The Churchill Factor, 2014.

On Churchill's rhetorical skills in getting his point across.

- *noun* a striking or amusing remark; from American baseball slang for a 'fastball' pitch
- see also **anaphora, chiasmus, dash of Dawson, epiphenomena, funky Gibbon, Gibbonian, megalopsychia, numen, orotund, runty kid, selfish tosser, skull-piling warlord, syllogism, transmogrifying, wangled, Zeus and Polyhymnia**

Zoink

'The excitement is growing so much I think the Geiger counter of Olympo-mania is going to go zoink off the scale.'
27 July 2012.

Speaking on the eve of the London Olympics.

- interjection, exclamation of surprise or shock; from 'zoinks!', popularised by US cartoon character Scooby Doo
- see also **eudaimonia, gobsmacked, Pindaric, switcheroo, wet otters**

Zonk

'Marina and I meet up and we go for some zonk at Swyncombe.'
Friends, Voters, Countrymen, 2001.

Getting some rest with wife Marina Wheeler in Swyncombe, a pretty village near his Henley constituency.

- *noun* heavy sleep; 1940s, imitative
- see also **black abyss, ils sont passes, ces beaux jours, matricide,
  Morpheus, parable of the toast, scrumple, stumblebum**

BIBLIOGRAPHY

Dale, Iain and Szweda, Jakub, *The Big Book of Boris* (London: Biteback, 2019)

Gimson, Andrew, *Boris: The Adventures of Boris Johnson* (London: Simon & Schuster, 2016)

— —, *Boris: The Rise of Boris Johnson* (London: Simon & Schuster, 2006)

Johnson, Boris, *The Churchill Factor: How One Man Made History* (London: Hodder & Stoughton, 2014)

— —, *The Dream of Rome* (London: HarperCollins, 2006)

— —, *Friends, Voters, Countrymen: Jottings on the Stump* (London: HarperCollins, 2001)

— —, *Have I Got Views For You* (London: Harper Perennial, 2006)

— —, *Johnson's Life of London: The People Who Made the City That Made the World* (London: HarperPress, 2011)

— —, *Lend Me Your Ears* (London: HarperCollins, 2003)

— —, *Life in The Fast Lane: The Johnson Guide to Cars* (London: Harper Perennial, 2007)

— —, *Seventy-Two Virgins* (London: HarperCollins, 2004)

— —, *The Spirit of London* (London: HarperCollins, 2012)

Mount, Harry, *The Wit and Wisdom of Boris Johnson* (London: Bloomsbury, 2013)

Purnell, Sonia, *Just Boris: The Irresistible Rise of a Political Celebrity* (London: Aurum Press, 2011)

ACKNOWLEDGEMENTS

T hanks to everyone at Biteback for their hard work. I'm grateful to Ellen Heaney and Owen Bennett for their research, and to Asa Bennett for his thorough checking of the classical references.

ACKNOWLEDGMENTS